W9-AEP-891

PRESENTING

Robert Lipsyte

Twayne's United States Authors Series
Young Adult Authors

Patricia J. Campbell, General Editor

TUSAS 649

ROBERT LIPSYTE

PRESENTING
Robert Lipsyte

Michael Cart

Twayne Publishers
An Imprint of Simon & Schuster Macmillan
New York

Prentice Hall International
London Mexico City New Delhi Singapore Sydney

Acknowledgment is gratefully made to those publishers and individuals who permitted the use of the following photographs in copyright.

p. 18 photograph by Bert Silverman, courtesy of *New York Times* Pictures; p. 19 photograph courtesy of AP/WIDE WORLD PHOTOS; p. 21 photograph courtesy of *New York Times* Pictures; p. 103 photograph by and courtesy of Kate Kunz

Twayne United States Authors Series No. 649

Presenting Robert Lipsyte
Michael Cart

Twayne Publishers
An Imprint of Simon & Schuster Macmillan
866 Third Avenue
New York, NY 10022

Library of Congress Cataloging-in-Publication Data

Cart, Michael.
    Presenting Robert Lipsyte / Michael Cart.
       p.   cm. — (Twayne's young adult author series)
    Includes bibliographical references and index.
    ISBN 0–8057–4151–8
    1. Lipsyte. Robert—Criticism and interpretation.   2. Young adult fiction, American—History and criticism.   [1. Lipsyte, Robert—Criticism and interpretation.   2. American literature—History and criticism.]   I. Title.   II. Series.
PS3562.I64Z63   1995
813'.54—dc20   94–44520
                                                                                        CIP
                                                                                        AC

The paper used in this publication meets the minimum requirements of American National Standard for Information Sciences—Permanence of Paper for Printed Library Materials, ANSI Z39.48-1984. ∞ ™

Printed in the United States of America.

10 9 8 7 6 5 4 3 2 1

Contents

Foreword

The advent of Twayne's Young Adult Author Series in 1985 was a response to the growing stature and value of adolescent literature and the lack of serious critical evaluation of the new genre. The first volume of the series was heralded as marking the coming-of-age of young adult fiction.

The aim of the series is twofold. First, it enables young readers to research the work of their favorite authors and to see them as real people. Each volume is written in a lively, readable style and attempts to present in an attractive, accessible format a vivid portrait of the author as a person.

Second, the series provides teachers and librarians with insights and background material for promoting and teaching young adult novels. Each of the biocritical studies is a serious literary analysis of one author's work (or one subgenre within young adult literature), with attention to plot structure, theme, character, setting, and imagery. In addition, many of the series writers delve deeper into the creative writing process by tracking down early drafts or unpublished manuscripts by their subject authors, consulting with their editors or other mentors, and examining influences from literature, film, or social movements.

Many of the authors contributing to the series are among the leading scholars and critics of adolescent literature. Some are even novelists for young adults themselves. Each study is based on extensive interviews with the subject author and an exhaustive study of his or her work. Although the general format is the same, the individual volumes are uniquely shaped by their subjects, and each brings a different perspective to the classroom.

The goal of the series is to produce a succinct but comprehensive study of the life and art of every leading writer for young adults to trace how that art has been accepted by readers and critics, and to evaluate its place in the developing field of adolescent literature. And—perhaps most important—the series is intended to inspire a reading and rereading of this quality fiction that speaks so directly to young people about their life's experiences.

PATRICIA J. CAMPBELL, GENERAL EDITOR

Preface

On a crisp, clear day in early March 1993 I interviewed Robert Lipsyte at his two-story apartment near Union Square on Manhattan's Lower East Side. Though initially wary—no one is more suspicious of an interviewer than another interviewer—Lipsyte quickly warmed up to questions about his work, especially when we moved downstairs to the cheerfully cluttered room where he does his writing.

To engage Lipsyte in conversation is to be impressed by his obvious intelligence, wit, and the quickness of a mind that produces ideas, some of them contradictory, at a prodigious rate. Though he denies being particularly introspective (when I asked him about thematic considerations, he grinned and replied, "With all due respect that's why they're paying YOU the big bucks!"), his conversation becomes a kind of thinking-out-loud dialectic that demonstrates his grasp and comprehension of more sides to issues than most people know exist. It is this mental felicity and facility that may explain why only part of his creative life has been directed to writing young adult books. Indeed, he is surely the only author for young adults to have won an Emmy Award as host of his own PBS television program!

Consider that in addition to being a celebrated writer for young adults, Lipsyte has also been a distinguished reporter (*Newsweek* magazine called him "the most original and elegant writer on the sports staff of the *New York Times*), a newspaper and magazine columnist, a screenwriter, an adult novelist, an author of nonfiction books for both adults and young adults, and a television essayist, commentator, and correspondent.

Lipsyte professes some confusion about this professional plethora. While asserting that "as long as I can remember, the only thing I ever seriously wanted to be was a writer," he goes on to admit, "What was never clear, and what is still not clear at fifty-five, is what kind of writer. Am I a screenwriter? (I have movies produced.) Am I a young adult writer? An "old adult" writer? A journalist? I don't know what I am. I think," he concludes wryly, "I'm just kind of a hired writer."

This is nicely disingenuous, but it does him a disservice, for whatever else he may be Lipsyte is inarguably a seminal figure in modern young adult literature. His first novel, *The Contender*, published in 1967, helped set the stage for realistic novels of social conscience and relevance to the lives of young readers. In the twenty-six years since its publication the book has grown in critical reputation and popularity: its publisher, HarperCollins, reports that more than 1,585,000 copies have been sold.

In this book and the seven other novels that have followed it, Lipsyte has grappled with such timeless themes as the individual's redeeming power for self-transformation, the importance of individual social conscience, and the meaning of manhood, castigating, in the latter regard, the "Rocky" myth, male sexism, and the societal tendency to treat boys "as a group, a pack, herd, team, gang, or board of directors instead of as individuals." His writing has been enriched by this ongoing dialectic, particularly in its expansive characterization and its overriding compassion.

Lipsyte remains one of a handful of young adult authors (S. E. Hinton, Robert Cormier, and Paul Zindel are others) who transformed teenage fiction into a viable body of modern literature for young adults, serious novels dealing realistically with the kinds of hard-edged issues that confront and challenge young people on their troubled journey from adolescence to adulthood. The problems that Lipsyte addresses in his fiction are organic to his plots, never artificially imposed on them, and his characters are complex and fully realized, never convenient clichés or thematic props. If they are often contenders, their creator, Robert Lipsyte, is inarguably a champion of the young adult novel.

I am, of course, grateful to Robert Lipsyte for his cordial cooperation and candor, for his patience in answering my sometimes undigested questions, and for taking time from a prodigiously busy schedule to talk at length with me about his life and work.

Chronology

1938   Robert Michael Lipsyte is born in New York City on 16 January.

1952   Takes summer job as a lawn boy and loses forty pounds.

1957   Graduates from Columbia College. Begins work as copy boy in the sports department of the *New York Times*.

1959   Receives M.A. from Columbia University School of Journalism. Becomes sports reporter for the *New York Times*. Marries Maria Glaser.

1962   Begins covering New York Mets, his first major assignment.

1963   First marriage ends in divorce.

1964   *Nigger* (coauthored with Dick Gregory). Begins covering boxing for the *New York Times* and meets Cassius Clay (later Muhammad Ali). Wins Dutton Best Sports Story Award.

1965   Wins Dutton Best Sports Story Award.

1966   *The Masculine Mystique*. Wins Mike Berger Award for Distinguished Reporting. Marries Marjorie Rubin, a novelist.

1967   *The Contender*. Becomes sports columnist for the *New York Times*. Wins Dutton Best Sports Story Award.

1968   Son Sam is born on 21 June. *The Contender* wins Child
Study Association's Wel-Met Children's Book Award and
is named ALA Notable Book for Children.

1970   *Assignment: Sports.*

1971   Leaves the *New York Times.* Daughter Susannah is born
on 14 January. Wins Dutton Best Sports Story Award.
The Contender is named an ALA Notable Book for
Children 1940–1970.

1973   *Something Going* (with Steve Cady).

1974   *Liberty Two.*

1975   *SportsWorld: An American Dream. That's the Way of the
World* (screenplay).

1976   Wins Dutton Best Sports Story Award. Becomes commentator for National Public Radio.

1977   *One Fat Summer.* Becomes columnist for the *New York
Post. One Fat Summer* is named a *New York Times* Best
Book of the Year.

1978   *Free to Be Muhammad Ali.* Diagnosed with cancer. New
Jersey Author Citation from New Jersey Institute of
Technology.

1981   *Summer Rules.*

1982   *The Summerboy. Jock and Jill.* Leaves National Public
Radio. Becomes sports essayist for *CBS Sunday Morning.
The Summerboy* is named Booklist Editors' Choice.

1984   Revised edition of *Assignment: Sports.*

1986   Leaves CBS. Becomes sports correspondent for NBC
News.

1987   Second marriage ends.

1988   Leaves NBC News.

1989 Becomes host of *The Eleventh Hour* on PBS. *One Fat Summer* named ALA Best of the Best Books for Young Adults, 1966–1988.

1990 Wins Emmy Award for On-Camera Achievement. *The Eleventh Hour* is canceled after two seasons.

1991 *The Brave.* Resumes sports column for the *New York Times.* Diagnosed with cancer for the second time.

1992 *The Chemo Kid.* Begins column for *American Health.* *The Brave* named an ALA Best Book for Young Adults and an ALA Recommended Book for Reluctant Young Adult Readers. Marries Katherine L. Sulkes, a television producer.

1993 *The Chief. Jim Thorpe: 20th Century Jock. Arnold Schwarzenegger: Hercules in America.* "Coping" column for the *New York Times.*

1. Becoming a Contender

"I've had some really lucky, lucky experiences in my life and certainly *The Contender* was one of them."

—Robert Lipsyte

The tawdry, neon-lit streets and crowded casinos of Las Vegas, Nevada, seem an unlikely setting for the start of a celebrated career in writing books for young adults, but that is where it happened for Robert Lipsyte. The year was 1965, and Lipsyte, only twenty-seven but already a noted sportswriter for the *New York Times*, was in town to cover the heavyweight boxing title bout between Muhammad Ali and Floyd Patterson. At loose ends the night before the 22 November fight, Lipsyte found himself sitting by a deserted hotel swimming-pool, listening to an old fight manager reminisce, never dreaming that the stories he was hearing would add a new dimension to his life and enrich the changing world of literature for young adults.

The manager was Cus D'Amato. Though he was only in his late fifties, he seemed much older to Lipsyte, and it was obvious that his glory days were behind him. "His influence within the sport was gone," Lipsyte asserts. "He had trained champions. Now he buttonholed strangers."[1] But this particular stranger found the older man's reminiscences fascinating, particularly the story of how D'Amato used to sit in his gym on New York's Lower East Side, waiting to hear the sound of footsteps on the three flights of steep stairs outside. "If a kid came up those dark, narrow, twisting flights of stairs alone and running scared," Lipsyte remembers D'Amato telling him, "there was a chance he might stay with it, hang tough, find himself through dedication and sacrifice." What

1

the older man said next reverberated in Lipsyte's imagination: "Fear," according to D'Amato, is "like fire. It can burn you or keep you warm; it can destroy you or make you a hero, a contender in the ring and in life."[2] "I sat up the rest of that night aflame," Lipsyte recalls. "To me becoming a contender meant writing a novel" ("Facets," 16).

Although Lipsyte had already published one nonfiction book for adults (he coauthored black comedian and political activist Dick Gregory's 1964 autobiography *Nigger*), he had always been "afraid" (his word) to try his hand at a novel, for fear he had nothing to say. But now he realized that D'Amato's story was a match that had set his imagination afire with images and ideas and questions.

Life is seldom as tidy and structured as art, but what happened next seems, in retrospect, to have an almost novelistic inevitability. Returning to New York after the fight (which Ali won), Lipsyte discovered a letter waiting for him from Ferd Monjo, then an editor at Harper and Row Junior Books. In the letter Monjo complimented the sportswriter on his boxing coverage and then got to the point: had he ever thought about writing a novel with the ring as its milieu?

Had he! Lipsyte recalls phoning Monjo immediately and pouring out the ideas his imagination was forming about a young black man climbing the stairs to a gym to become a contender. With no more than a verbal "go-ahead" from Monjo, Lipsyte sat down and wrote the story that would become his first novel, *The Contender*.

Ironically Lipsyte knew nothing about young adult literature as a genre when he published this first novel. Writing about the novel's creation some years later, he noted, "Because the novel was short and linear, sexless—though violent—and the protagonist was seventeen years old, it was packaged for a newly created market: Young Adult, Ages 12-and-up" ("Listening," 293). In fact, it is not completely accurate to say that this was a "newly created" market, since books for teenagers had been an identifiable genre (or market) for decades, at least since the publication of Maureen Daly's *Seventeenth Summer* in 1942. What did set it apart was a quality it shared with another important book published in the landmark year of 1967: S. E. Hinton's *The Outsiders*. Both books dealt, in their unflinching realism, with the real-life problems of protagonists who, perhaps for the first time, were not privileged, prom-going, college-bound, crew-cut, middle-class adolescents but—well, *outsiders* instead: Hinton's Oklahoma "greasers" and Lipsyte's African-American teens who walked Harlem's mean streets. Together these two books ushered in what Alleen Pace Nilsen and Kenneth L. Donelson call, in their standard study *Literature for Today's Young Adults*, "the new realism." Though Lipsyte was not at the time conscious that he was a kind of creative midwife delivering a new age of more realistic, and hence more relevant, literature for young readers, the form and style of novel he had instinctively chosen to write make perfect retrospective sense. After all, by 1967 he had been a sports reporter for the *New York Times* for eight years and had developed a reporter's eye for closely observed detail and a journalist's allegiance to telling the unflinching and often unpleasant truth. In the same year that *The Contender* was published, Lipsyte became a columnist for the *Times* and quickly demonstrated in his columns that, as a journalist, he was much more interested in the novelist's "who" and "why" than the reporter's more straightforward "when, where, and what."

All of this becomes abundantly clear on reading his first novel. His "contender" is Alfred Brooks, a seventeen-year-old African-American who lives with his widowed Aunt Pearl and her three small daughters in a tiny Harlem apartment. Alfred is an orphan, deserted, at the age of ten, by his father and robbed of his mother by her death from pneumonia when he was thirteen. A high-school dropout, Alfred is working as a stockboy in a neighborhood grocery and is jeeringly referred to by the neighborhood street kids as "Good Old Uncle Alfred." The reader may infer—though the author does not explicitly say so—that this is, in part, an insulting reference to "Uncle Tom," since Alfred's employers, the three Epstein brothers, are white. It is also an unflattering reference (from the other kids' point of view) to Alfred's "straightness": even though his is a dead-end job, he is the only one in his circle of teenage acquaintances who is employed, and he dutifully gives his weekly wages to his aunt. His idea of a good time is the escapist pleasure of going to the movies with his only friend, James, who, it will develop, is a heroin addict. And, finally, it refers to Alfred's ambitionless life. His upwardly mobile, college-student cousin Jeff puts it this way: "You always seemed so . . . so negative. . . . You sort of seemed to . . . just drift along."[3]

Lipsyte establishes Alfred's oppressively enervating environment on the very first page through references to "the dirty gray Harlem sky," "the sour air," "the garbage and broken glass" in the streets, the "packs of little kids, raggedy and skinny, [who] raced past him along the gutter's edge, kicking empty beer cans ahead of them" (1). Searching for James, who has failed to show up for a movie date, Alfred finds him in a neighborhood clubroom with three members of a street gang ("those worthless punks," Aunt Pearl has called them). The clubroom, with its broken-down furniture, "scratchy records," "cracked mirrors," and "naked light bulbs" is as depressing as the streets. Alfred is understandably anxious to escape to the dreamy sanctuary of the movies with James, but instead finds himself forced to defend his white employers.

When the bullying Major sneers, "How much them Jews give you for slavin'," Alfred weakly replies that they treat him "all right" (3), but then, in an awkward attempt to praise their devoutness, he inadvertently reveals that the Epsteins refuse to touch money after sundown on Friday (the beginning of their Sabbath) and thus have left the day's cash receipts in the cash register. Major and his cohorts decide to rob the store, and when Alfred refuses to accompany them, they taunt him: "You just a slave. You was born a slave. You gonna die a slave" (4).

It is not this questionable indictment that hurts Alfred, but rather his inability to dissuade James from accompanying the others. His pain and self-loathing are exacerbated when he later realizes that he has failed to warn the would-be robbers of the new burglar alarm his employers have installed and has thus put his only friend in jeopardy. And, indeed, when the alarm is inevitably tripped and the police are summoned, it is James who is captured, while the others flee to beat Alfred unconscious when they find him on his way home.

Sufficiently recovered by the next evening to wander dispirited-ly about the neighborhood streets, Alfred comes across a group of buildings and notices, on the third floor of one of them, a window with the faded letters "Donatelli's gym" painted on it. He dimly remembers his father telling him that Joe Louis and Sugar Ray Robinson had worked out there once and, bitterly recalling Major's jeering indictment of him, thinks, "They weren't no slaves and they didn't have to bust into anybody's grocery store. They made it, they got to be somebody" (19).

He then sees a figure approaching, which he thinks is Major, and darts across the street in terror—almost being run down by traffic in the process. This triggers a moment of dazzling epiphany, as he realizes that what ultimately will enslave him is not working for the white man but, instead, giving in to his own fear. Feeling "a ball of ice" (a combination of fear and adrenaline) forming "in the pit of his stomach," he slowly, haltingly, but res-olutely begins climbing the three flights of worn wooden steps. At the top he will meet Mr. Donatelli (Cus D'Amato's fictionalized alter ego) and begin the slow and painful process of transforming himself from "Good Old Uncle Alfred" into a contender.

For Donatelli (and for Lipsyte) the word "contender" has an almost talismanic value. When Alfred explains that he wants to be "Somebody special. A Champion," Donatelli's thin lips tighten. "Everybody wants to be a champion," he snorts. "That's not enough. You have to start by wanting to be a contender, the man coming up, the man who knows there's a good chance he'll never get to the top, the man who's willing to sweat and bleed to get up as high as his legs and his brains and his heart will take him" (25).

The three flights of stairs Alfred has climbed to get this far have thus an added symbolic value. They can carry him, through strenuous climbing, to the brink of opportunity or—midway through the book when his determination flags and he climbs to the gym to tell Mr. Donatelli he is giving up—to the edge of fail-ure. In bringing Alfred to the gym, Lipsyte has established him-self as a powerful writer with a marvelous gift for economy. In only nineteen pages, he has managed to create a keenly observed and fully realized world, to introduce virtually all of his major characters, to provide them with believable motivations and to establish a transcendent theme—self-transformation—strong enough to support his evolving narrative.

The overarching theme of self-transformation will also impact and interact with a secondary theme: friendship and both the life-enlarging opportunities it offers and the responsibilities it imposes. It is obvious that Alfred's relationship with his lifelong friend James is the most important element in his life. The reader quickly understands that James is the stronger partner in the friendship. It is Alfred, after all, who must nervously wait for a friend who is typically, and perhaps thoughtlessly, late when they plan to go to the movies. It is Alfred who must then go in search of the friend and remind him of their plans, even though the movies are a Friday-night fixture of their lives. Understanding this inequity, Alfred thinks, resentfully, "What am I, James' shadow or something? I don't need him" (2).

But everything in Alfred's attitude and conduct betrays to the reader that this is self-delusion. Alfred *does* need James. Though they are the same age, James has been more like an older brother, supporting Alfred through the loss of his parents, entertaining him with his imitations of their school's principal. It is James who has discovered the cave in Central Park that became their childhood sanctuary and refuge from the world—and tellingly, it is James who stays at the front of the cave keeping watch against danger, while Alfred cowers at the back. It is James who tries to persuade Alfred to stay in school. It is James who is ambitious, planning to be an engineer and build things, spinning dreams for Alfred of their working together, making a fortune and driving back to the neighborhood in a white Cadillac "right to the cave," where they would "crawl on the ground in their silk suits, and pull out any little kids they found in there and buy them something really fine" (10–11).

And yet it is James who, four months after Alfred has dropped out of school, drops out himself and begins hanging out with the street gang, accepting, without argument, their claim that "the white man would never let him [James] build anything but garbage heaps" (11). James's dropping out of school and society destroys Alfred's dreams of a prosperous future, for at this stage in his life it would never occur to him that he could build his own future independently. In fact, when James is captured trying to rob the grocery store and is imprisoned, Alfred lies in bed reflecting miserably on the loss of his friendship and, by extension, his future: "*Was* my best friend. No partner, nothing. Stay in bed. . . . Just stay in bed, man, until you're eighteen, then join the Army. No, stay in bed forever" (15).

The loss of his friend is doubly devastating to Alfred, who, having forgotten to warn James of the Epsteins' new burglar alarm, blames himself for his erstwhile friend's arrest. And James, who refuses to accept responsibility for anything and therefore needs regular recourse to a scapegoat, is happy to collude with Alfred in this belief. Ultimately, as Alfred begins to transform himself through boxing and the self-discipline it imposes, the nature of the friendship is transformed, too. As Alfred climbs higher up the contender's steps, James slips lower and lower into the depths of drug addiction until, at the book's end, the original roles are completely reversed. Alfred is now the strong one. Finding James, who has been wounded in another attempt to rob the Epsteins' store, bleeding and cowering in their cave, Alfred insists he can help with his redemption—with getting clean, getting a job, and turning his life around. James asks, "Why you wanna do all this?" Alfred's answer is both telling and touching: "Because I know I can, James. And you're my partner" (166). Obviously being a contender means having the courage and inner strength to help not only yourself but a friend as well.

Alfred's transformation is beautifully and believably dramatized by Lipsyte. Alfred's climb to contention is never assured: there are stumbles and missteps owing to his self-doubt, inner conflicts, and continuing anxiety about James. In fact, it is Alfred's desire to see James again that leads him back to the clubroom six weeks after his first visit and to a dramatic turning point in his progress toward becoming a contender.

James is not in the clubroom when Alfred arrives, but a party is in progress. Killing time until his former friend arrives, Alfred joins the party, reluctantly at first, then more spiritedly as he begins to drink wine and share the marijuana cigarettes being passed around. By the time James shows up the next morning, Alfred is in a semi-helpless state somewhere between intoxication and hangover. James is now clearly addicted to heroin—"The round face was thin, the eyes sunken" (88)—and, in fact, has come to the clubroom only to get a fix. Alfred tries desperately but ineffectively to persuade him not to take the drug but passes out instead, hearing James dismiss their friendship as "kid stuff" (89).

The next day the weekend assumes even more nightmarish qualities. Alfred finds himself on a joyride with Major in a stolen white Cadillac convertible—a nicely ironic comment on the perversion of his and James's childhood fantasy, which now, too, seems to be "kid stuff." At the end of a hideous day, Alfred, filled with self-loathing at what he perceives to be his failure to help James, goes to the gym to clear out his locker and give up boxing. But he cannot resist haltingly asking Mr. Donatelli if he could have become a contender. "Don't ask me," Donatelli replies. "Then who?" Alfred asks. "Yourself. Anyone can be taught how to fight. A contender, that you have to do yourself" (102).

It is the answer Alfred desperately needs to hear. A crisis is averted. A corner is turned. And Alfred returns to the ring with renewed determination and the emerging understanding that boxing, and becoming a contender, are more than dazzling combinations and fancy footwork. They also are something that Donatelli now sees in Alfred: "You're thinking," he says approvingly (106). And, indeed, Alfred is now developing his mind as well as his body, thinking and learning. "The more you learn, the more you want to know," another character, Bill ("Spoon") Witherspoon, says (118).

Spoon is an intriguing character. A former protégé of Mr. Donatelli's, he has left the ring, gone back to school, and become a teacher. His apartment, where Alfred rests before fights, is filled with books and a vision of a life that Alfred might someday lead. Spoon is a born teacher (ruefully acknowledging that he loves to lecture) and, perhaps more than any other character, is a surrogate and spokesperson for Lipsyte himself, who is also a self-acknowledged lecturer ("I lecture my children," he grins, "and I lecture my wife. And I lecture my friends. I'm always kind of declaiming.")[4]

This is not to say that *The Contender* is a didactic work, although it does offer lessons in the context of its fictional framework. But it is to say that the work is very serious-minded, like Alfred himself, and has a strong thematic purpose. In a recent interview, Lipsyte cautiously allowed that if there is a theme that unifies the body of his work, it is the process of "becoming." Alfred, when the reader first meets him, is not a fully formed person, for, as a teenager, he is still in the process of becoming an adult. One of the strengths of *The Contender* is the believability of Alfred's growth as a character as he continues his own process of becoming. At the outset he is like Fred Bauer in Lipsyte's later novel, *The Chemo Kid*: "He was here. We think."[5]

"You just always been so closed into yourself, Alfred," Aunt Pearl points out (132). For Alfred the process of becoming is one of unfolding, of opening up. Instead of being enervating, the process of life becomes exciting. Here is Aunt Pearl again: "You never been excited about anything in your life till today" (72). While Alfred will never be exactly lighthearted, his essential gravity is now lightened by flashes of appealing humor, usually expressed as affectionate banter with Aunt Pearl.

Lipsyte recognizes that as a character engaged in the process of becoming, Alfred has much in common with his readers. Speaking of authors like himself, Lipsyte muses, "You are feeding in information to a mind that's still changing and becoming and growing; you have a real responsibility not to feed in lies and take it in directions that are not true." He thinks for a moment and then concludes, "I guess that's the only rule: don't lie to kids."

The reader senses that Spoon, too, would never lie to Alfred. Nor would Mr. Donatelli. Indeed, the day will come when the manager will tell Alfred the hard-edged truth: that he does not have the killer instinct necessary to become a professional fighter and that it is time to retire. There was a time when Alfred would have meekly accepted this judgment. But not now. Now he has *learned* too much about himself and his possibilities to retire before he learns one last thing. He insists that he be permitted to finish his boxing career on his own terms—that is, getting into the ring for a final fight with a boxer who is good enough to hurt him, really hurt him, and thus to discover whether he has become a contender.

Alfred does fight that last fight, with courage and dignity, but he is defeated (this is a realistic novel, not a *Rocky* movie perpetuating the myth, which Lipsyte deplores, that sports is a ticket out of the ghetto). Yet in defeat he knows, without Mr. Donatelli's having to tell him, that he has made his climb, that he has become a contender, a fact he goes on to confirm, as previously noted, by resolving to help James. Moreover, he resolves to go to night school to learn how to help little kids, too, not by driving up in a white Cadillac and buying them something but by working in a neighborhood recreation center.

It is clearly intended to be a realistically cautious, optimistic ending. And Lipsyte is still angry, twenty-six years after publication of the book, about a well-known reviewer who, he feels, attacked him by implying that as a white author, he had no right to offer hope to blacks in the society of that time (or, as the reviewer put it, "where the rules of the game and the odds are set by distant outside societal forces").[6]

The hope Lipsyte offers to Alfred goes beyond considerations of race and social circumstance; it is, essentially, the universal hope that derives from the operation of free will in the arena of human choice. It is Alfred's power of free will that enables him to transcend his circumstances and that drives the book's theme of self-transformation in the milieu of the ring. Capitulation to straitened circumstances is also, of course, a "choice," and Lipsyte vividly dramatizes these possibilities. Alfred could have continued to drift along, seeking temporary relief from the dead-end reality of his life in the fantasy world of movies, or, like James, in the more dangerous escape of drugs; or he could have chosen a life of petty crime, like Major and the other gang members. He could have found equally mind-numbing sanctuary in the platitudes of Aunt Pearl's church, or he could have found a strident new self-identity through joining the black nationalists who harangue him from street corners. He could even have accepted his self-satisfied Uncle Wilson's advice to look for a career in the trades. To have selected any of these other "options," however, would have meant allowing other persons or forces to impose an identity on him. And so it is a natural expression of the book's theme that Alfred should, instead, have chosen to re-create himself by becoming a contender.

Inevitably this raises the larger question, in the context of the politically correct world of the 1990s, of the viability of a white author's writing about African-American characters. Lipsyte himself is ambivalent about this. As long ago as 1983, he told one interviewer, "In retrospect I'm appalled at my arrogance that I could have (written about a black protagonist), I'm not so sure I should have."[7] More recently he explained why he chose to write *The Contender* in the third person rather than in Alfred's own first-person voice: "I wasn't sure I had the technique, the craft to be totally true to a character who was that divorced from my own experience, although I felt that I could be true to a lot of the feelings that would be generic adolescent feelings." On the other hand, Lipsyte continues to powerfully believe that literature is "art" and in *that* context "you can do anything you want. I would never suggest that women can't write about men or whites about blacks." However, he does strongly believe that in such a case the writer "has a moral responsibility . . . to get it right."

Looking at Lipsyte's life prior to *The Contender*, one finds that a strong case can be made for claiming he had both the education and experience in writing and life "to get it right." For starters, both of his parents were teachers in the racially mixed Harlem and Bedford-Stuyvesant neighborhoods of New York City, and he went to their schools as a boy. "I've always been of the world," he recalls, "and as a journalist, I was out on the street a lot. So I think it's very hard not to be aware of what's happening." In addition, Lipsyte spent nine intense months in 1963–1964 with Dick Gregory while he was coauthoring the black comedian and political activist's autobiography. According to Lipsyte, Gregory was "one of the first of my really important street teachers. He took me into another world and gave me the beginning of an idea of what it means to be black in America . . . to really know what it feels like . . . to live in his world and in his skin and to meet his brothers and sisters. It was kind of wonderful; we came to understanding."

This "intense" (his word) experience with Gregory was followed by the early years of covering Muhammad Ali (then Cassius Clay) both in and out of the ring. "One experience informed the other," he notes, explaining that it was Gregory who initially helped him in terms of writing about black boxers and "feeling comfortable about going home with them" as part of their entourage, often as the only white member. He recalls the experience: "Sometimes it was a little scary; I mean, sometimes you feel like the problem or you feel isolated. Sometimes you are the pet and you have warm, jolly jokes . . . a lot of it was fun and there were times when I would have to look at the back of my hand to remind myself that I wasn't one of them."

In retrospect, Lipsyte feels such experiences were liberating for him as a writer, since they enabled him to recognize the reality behind the generic stereotypes of race and to write about blacks—and whites—as individuals, some good, some bad—like Major or Stick, the black antagonist of the later novel *The Brave*. On the other hand, Lipsyte has been criticized for including only sympathetic (that is, "good") white characters in *The Contender*. Yet the sociological reality of the 1960s would dictate that the fight trainer, Donatelli, be white (Ali's first trainer was also white, as, of course, was D'Amato, Floyd Patterson's trainer), and that Alfred's employers would also be white, as well as the policemen whom he encounters patroling the streets. Beyond this, the point should be made that the police are suspicious of Alfred when they first encounter him running in the early morning and are therefore unsympathetic authority figures (he is training, but they do not know that). And similarly, the Epsteins are suspicious of Alfred after his friends attempt to rob them, no longer trusting him to take their daily cash deposit to the bank. Alfred must prove himself to them, even as he begins to prove himself to himself.

If questions remain about the authenticity of the black teenager's world portrayed in the book, there is no argument about the absolute authenticity of the boxing scenes and the milieu of the ring. The scenes at the gym, in the pre- and post-fight locker rooms, and in the ring itself have the visceral power of detail so closely observed that the reader *knows* the author has been there, watching with a reporter's eye. Lipsyte covered boxing for four years for the *Times* and recalls, in his book *Assignment Sports*, "I never wrote so many stories so fast as during the four years that boxing was my beat. Writing under deadline is often exhilarating, and if you're lucky and the event has moved you, a rhythm develops and the story just flows out of your typewriter."[8] The rhythmic flow of Lipsyte's blow-by-blow descriptions of Alfred's fights propels the reader into the ring, and as the pace of the fight quickens, Lipsyte accelerates the pace of his narrative, too, moving naturally into a stream-of-consciousness technique.

Equally powerful is his portrayal of the crowd, which is like a ravenous predator in its insatiable desire for blood and pain. And then there are the fighters themselves: some are as predatory as the crowds; some are cocky; some are frightened; some are confident; some, doubtful; some are "rough and dirty in the clinches." Some are winners, some losers, some killers, and some victims. Some are black. Some are white. What they all have in common is that they bleed. And the thoughtful ones, like Spoon, find a larger meaning in this elementary fact of biology: "Once I found out that white boys bled the same color I did I figured I'd let them move into my neighborhood any time" (119).

As a novel, *The Contender* is many things: a compellingly readable sports story, a coming-of-age novel, a bildungsroman, a dramatic exposition of man's capacity for self-transformation, a social document. But, perhaps most lastingly, it is a tribute to the power of friendship and a celebration of brotherhood. It is also a testimonial to Lipsyte's own compassionate heart and social conscience. In each of these ways the novel inarguably established Lipsyte as a contender in the ring of young adult literature.

Yet nine years would pass before he wrote another novel for young adults.

2. Becoming Robert Lipsyte

"I think I'm just kind of a hired writer."

"Hired writer" Robert Lipsyte was born in New York City on 16 January 1938. He grew up in Queens, one of the five boroughs of New York City, in a neighborhood called Rego Park, which he has described as one of "attached houses, six-story apartment buildings, and many vacant jungly lots."[1] For a man who grew up to become one of America's most celebrated (and occasionally controversial) sportswriters, sports itself seems to have played little part in his boyhood, although he is ambivalent about how big that small part was. For one thing, as he has noted, "There was no great sporting tradition in the neighborhood, few organized sports of any kind" (*SportsWorld*, 3). For another, he was quite fat as a boy, "too fat for basketball," but "not fat enough to have my own zip code" ("Listening," 290).

And yet, when asked if sports had been a big part of his childhood, he first answers, immediately and forcefully, "No," but then pauses long enough for second thoughts. "Well," he says then, "I'm sure they were. They didn't *seem* to be at the time and they certainly didn't impinge on my consciousness, but growing up in the fifties when the tyranny of sports was routine in a striving, middle-class Jewish neighborhood, when boys really did find their identification in their bodies and if you didn't play sports, you were a 'fag,' or a 'sissy,' or a 'girl,'—yeah, as I think about it more and more, you know, I see how really important it all was." But then he adds an important distinction: "But in terms of did I know batting averages or did I give a shit whether the Yankees were winning, no! And I don't now. I never have. You know, it's rock and roll. It doesn't matter."

What did matter was the masquerade of caring that the tyranny of sports imposed on a fat boy like Lipsyte who *didn't* really care. (One measure of how little he really cared is that, though he grew up in a city that boasted three major league baseball teams, he did not attend a game until he was thirteen, and then, he recalls, "I was profoundly disappointed.") It is not wholly accurate to say it made him cynical about sports, but it did give him the distance necessary to look critically at competitive games and their implicit (and, he believes, meretricious) lesson that winning is everything and that if you lose, something is wrong with you. "Sports is a negative experience for most boys and almost all girls," he has stated flatly. "We force children to judge each other on their bodies, which is the thing everyone's most scared about. They're required to defend themselves on the basis of competitive physical ability."[2] As he wrote in his 1975 book *SportsWorld*, "Even for ballgames, these values . . . are not necessarily in the individual's best interests. But for daily life they tend to . . . socialize us for war or depression" (ix).

If Lipsyte felt pressure from his peers to parade an interest in sports, he felt none from his father, Sidney, a teacher, school administrator, and intellectual. (His mother, Fanny, was also a teacher.) "We had no sports relationship," Lipsyte recalls. "We went to one baseball game together our whole lives." Instead father and son went to the public library together, "at least once a week in the summertime, maybe more. I think our sports experience—you know, the father-playing-catch-with-the-son experience—was in the books: instead of a ball we (figuratively) threw books back and forth, talking about them."

Lipsyte does not recall reading sports books as a boy, even the critically acclaimed John R. Tunis ("I will discuss John R. Tunis at some length but I never read him as a kid. I'm sure I wouldn't have been too interested"). In fact, with the example and encouragement of his father, Lipsyte "graduated" at an early age from the library's children's room to its adult department, where he discovered the work of John Steinbeck, who would become a particular favorite of his. The adult Lipsyte is almost embarrassed by a question about the roots of his social conscience, thinking it makes him sound "too nice," but there is no doubt that his writing, both his sportswriting and his young adult novels, is largely informed by a Steinbeckian social consciousness. And significantly, his favorite writer as an adult is South African Nobel laureate Nadine Gordimer, who is noted for her own social conscience and stalwart opposition to apartheid.

Recalling his childhood, Lipsyte says, "The only thing I ever seriously wanted to be was a writer." Musing about what he calls the "prehistory" of this desire, he says, "Being a fat kid, I was unable to participate and so I became basically an observer of life." An observer and, one senses, an outsider, for "add to that," he continues, "the fact that both my parents were teachers, and so I had to wear a necktie to elementary school, which was, even then, pretty bizarre; it was like being the preacher's kid. And so, in many ways, I was watching rather than participating and that was my training for writing."

He was further distanced from his peers by his intelligence. "I was in something called The Special Progress Class—you know," he observes wryly, "those classes for the talented and fat." Later he was accepted into a Ford Foundation program that enabled him to go directly from his junior year at Forest Hills High School in Queens to the intellectually heady atmosphere of Columbia College. Thus, while he never officially graduated from high school, he did graduate from Columbia College as a nineteen-year-old English major in 1957. From there, he claims, he planned "to go to Hollywood, write novels and screenplays and be dissolute." If that were really his destination, the route he chose was more conventional: he enrolled at the prestigious Claremont Graduate School in Southern California.

But he never got there.

He recalls what happened instead: "Because I needed money, I got a summer job driving a horse-watering truck for the ASPCA." However, because the job ("which sounded kind of great") was not due to start for several weeks, Lipsyte, hoping for a tempo-

Lipsyte's bar mitzvah, 1951. With father, Sidney, mother, Fanny, and six-year-old sister, Gale.

rary job until then, answered an ad for an editorial assistant at the *New York Times*. As he recalls, the job interviewer reluctantly permitted him to fill out an application but was not encouraging, explaining, in snooty *Times* style, that "these jobs were for Rhodes Scholars and Ph.D. candidates." Lipsyte remembers going from the interview to "some Western movies in Times Square." After that he went home to Queens, "and as I walked in the door, my mother said, 'You've just gotten a crank call that you're to report to the *New York Times* tomorrow and if you pass your physical in the afternoon, you'll start to work that night.'"

Of course, it was not a crank call. He did pass the physical the next day, and he did get the job, which turned out to be that of copy boy in the sports department, running errands and carrying sportswriters' typed stories ("copy") from desk to desk. "And that's how I became a sportswriter," Lipsyte concludes. "I had no particular interest in sports otherwise." Or in journalism, for

The young reporter covering boxing at Shea Stadium, 1967. Photo by Bert Silverman, courtesy of the *New York Times*.

that matter. As previously noted, while Lipsyte had always wanted to be a writer, what he envisioned was not a career as a journalist but a Steinbeckian career as a novelist. But to his surprise, he quickly fell in love with what he calls "the romance of newspapering" and, after two years at the *Times*, returned to Columbia to earn a master's degree in journalism.

"It was a very exciting time at the *New York Times*, 1957, a time of tremendous change. They were trying to shake the 'great lady' image and so they had [hired] all these hot young reporters like Gay Talese—I was his copy boy—and were trying to make it a writer's paper. And in terms of being a writer in those days, there was no better place to be than the Sports Department. It was Dodge City; you could do anything you wanted." Encouraged and inspired at finding himself in "a writing culture," Lipsyte began free-lancing. "Every copy editor at the *Times* had an outside job," he recalls with a grin, "either writing for Street and Smith's *Chicks and Ammo Magazine* or the *Encyclopedia*

The reporter at ringside, 1971. Ali is down for the count.

Britannica. Within several months of being there, being a bright young college graduate, I was writing either learned dissertations on European handball for the *EB* (at nineteen I was the living expert on European handball, having never seen it played!) or articles about all-girl Amazon armies for *Chicks and Ammo.* It was probably about a year before I got anything in the paper itself, but I was a comer."

Lipsyte was obviously not the only one who thought so. After two years as a copy boy, he was promoted to become, at the age of twenty-one, perhaps the youngest reporter on the *Times* staff. After a three-year apprenticeship spent largely in the office at night, working as a rewrite man, Lipsyte got his first big break when sports editor James Roach sent him to Florida in the spring of 1962 to cover the then fledgling New York Mets base-ball team. At the time Lipsyte claims that he was not filled with social purpose. "I just wanted to get out there and see what was going on and write better stories about it than anyone else."

Two years after that, Lipsyte began covering boxing for the *Times*, meeting in the process a brash young boxer from Louisville, Kentucky, named Cassius Clay. He continued on that beat (finding the inspiration there for *The Contender*) until 1967, when his career took another great leap forward as he was named one of the two sports columnists for the *Times*. If it is true, as he claims, that he was devoid of social purpose as a young reporter, he found it in his new role as a columnist. Referring to the impact of civil rights, black power, and "jock power" on athletics, he says: "It was an exciting time to be writing a column, the newly surfaced turmoil in sports seemed a natural climate, more so since I was sharing the internationally syndicated column—"Sports of the Times"—with Arthur Dailey, whose approach was traditional, conservative, sentimentally nostalgic" (*SportsWorld*, 129). No wonder that, as Lipsyte notes, "We were perfect foils for each other."

Assignment Sports

A selection of Lipsyte's columns and the stories he had filed as a young reporter, from spring training and elsewhere, form the basis for his second book for young adults: not a novel this time, but instead a collection of sports pieces titled *Assignment Sports*, which was published by Harper and Row in 1970. These twenty-four short pieces (most are only three or four pages long) give an excellent sense of how very different Lipsyte was from most sportswriters of his time and establish his place among the "hot young reporters" to whom he has alluded. Do not expect to find a statistical rehash or a tired, play-by-play recounting of yesterday's game in these vignettes. What interests Lipsyte, instead, are the people who play the game and the fans who follow it; what they reveal about themselves in the conversations that Lipsyte, the attentive observer, carefully records; and the sometimes quirky, often offbeat and downright oddball moments that

Lord of the flies.
And punts.
And baskets.

This is Sports Columnist
Robert Lipsyte
of The New York Times.
He gets his innings
3 times a week.

Lipsyte, the columnist, 1971. Photo courtesy of the *New York Times*.

illuminate play and player alike. In his rejection of the conventions of sportswriting, in his choice of subject, his interest in character, and his borrowing of narrative techniques from the world of the fiction writer, Lipsyte, as one reviewer has pointed out, is a practitioner, like Gay Talese and Tom Wolfe, of the so-called "new Journalism."[3] Indeed, Talese himself has observed that Lipsyte brought "a smooth literary touch" to the *Times* sports page.

Certainly his choice of subject, which implicitly defines his idea of the meaning of the word "sports," is new, or at least nontraditional. Here are pieces, for example, about the World's Champion Eater, Bozo Miller, and about a fat little pug dog named "Dorold's Own Starlet II," whom we meet in the decidedly weird, behind-the-scenes world of the Westminster Dog Show. Here is saber champion Jack Keane, with his "great white smile" and his crisp black curls. And here is the once strongest man in the world, a Soviet weightlifter named Yuri Vlasov who, trying to hoist both a career in sport *and* newfound success as a writer, agonizes that "sport drains my energy and leaves nothing for writing" (85).

Lipsyte not only captures memorable moments and characters like these but also delivers memorable phrases. Here is how he describes another Soviet weightlifter, Leonid Zhabotinsky: "his golden-tipped curly hair glistening atop the mushy, mobile face that seemed to munch on itself—now sly, now terrified, always about to fall apart like raw marble beneath the chisel of a clumsy sculptor" (115). His prose style may lack the hot, idiosyncratic intensity of a Tom Wolfe, but in its use of similes and metaphors that are wonderfully consistent with his tone and subject, his voice attains the enduring resonance of the successful novelist or short-story writer.

Lipsyte matches his interest in characters with an uncanny ability to capture their essence, whether they are celebrities or wanna-bes who can only dream of fame and, perhaps, fortune. As for celebrities, here is golfing great Arnold Palmer, observed on a tournament fairway; he is smoking, "dragging on the cigarette as if it held the wind's secret, frowning down at the grass, flattening it with a glance." A police helicopter lands outside the golf course, "and Palmer scowled the whirling blades into silence" (65).

But Lipsyte is even better at capturing the essence of those who can only dream of success, like twenty-one-year-old John Pappas, who shows up at the Mets' Florida spring training camp in his "black pointy shoes" (5), determined to be a pitcher for the team. The author artfully shows us Pappas's hopes and aspirations, but he also gives us an emotionally moving picture of the fine line between dreams and self-delusion, first by showing how Pappas fails his tryout and then by leaving us with this picture: "The last time I saw John Pappas he was framed in the car window, and he said, 'You know, I'm sorry they didn't give me a chance to hit. I'm not a bad hitter. And I play the outfield, too'" (8).

What further sets Lipsyte apart from traditional sportswriting is his emotional mastery of his material. Many of these pieces are poignant and invite the reader's emotional involvement, but they never fall into the too-easy trap of sentimentality. One of the most memorable pieces in the book is about women wheelchair athletes who recognize the difficulty of writing about their situation and plead with Lipsyte, "Don't go back and write a sob sister story about us" (74). To his credit, he does not. And in telling moments like these, the reader realizes the truth of one reviewer's observation that *Assignment Sports* "shows a writer concerned about characters, what they think and feel and how they act in human circumstances. . . . The book makes it because finally you realize that only the background is sports" (Elkin, 14).

The book also succeeds as an enduring document because of Lipsyte's concern for and interest in the social context of sport, where, as he puts it, "politics, race, religion, money, the law—all play roles" (87). His understanding that "sports is no sanctuary from reality" is further evidence of his Steinbeckian social consciousness, which is most clearly demonstrated in the two longest pieces in the book: one about Muhammad Ali and the other about the controversial 1968 Olympic Games, the so-called "problem games." The two pieces are structured similarly: each offers a series of short "takes" or scenes that, cumulatively, show us the complexity not only of the people but of the issues involved as well.

Lipsyte's portrayal of Ali speaking to a political gathering in San Francisco, for example, and struggling to understand the conflict between his conservative religion, Islam, and the liberal politics of his audience gives the reader a thought-provoking insight not only into Ali's character but also into the temper of the troubled times. Similarly, his vignettes on the politically charged 1968 Olympics are a marvel of irony, a tone he establishes in his lead, where he quotes the then president of the International Olympic Committee, Avery Brundage: "At least there is one place in this troubled world free from politics, from religion, from racial prejudice" (94). He follows this immediately with a mini-profile of Harry Edwards, "tall and black and hard," a former discus thrower and basketball player, now a twenty-five-year-old sociology professor at California's San Jose State University and a political activist, who tells Lipsyte, "I think the time is gone when the black man is going to run and jump when the white man says so, and then come back home to run and jump some more to keep from being lynched" (95).

The ineluctable presence of politics is the leitmotif of all the vignettes that comprise this piece: the story of Steve Mokone from South Africa, the first black South African to play major league soccer in England; "The Party Line," in which a Soviet sports official muses about "the advantages of a socialistic system that gives possibilities to workers, students, and peasants to practice sport and go to the Olympic Games" (104). Or there is Lipsyte's portrayal of the underfunded, underprepared, overpowered Vietnamese team, whose "preparation for the Olympics was halted for five months by the Tet offensive of January, 1968" (110), but who are present at the games anyway, as one official tells Lipsyte, "to show the world that even a country at war is trying to normalize its life" (119). And there is the heartbreakingly smug presence of seventy-year-old Douglas Roby, president of the United States Olympic Committee, a white retired board chairman who, talking of "the black-white confrontation" at the games (this was the year when black medalists lowered their heads during the playing of the national anthem and raised their fists in the black power salute), tells Lipsyte, "When today's young people get to be thirty or thirty-five, they'll look back and see how foolish they were" (118).

Lipsyte concludes the piece with another ironic juxtaposing of Edwards and Brundage. Edwards comments, "Were there historic milestones? I don't know, but we turned over some rocks and saw what was underneath" (119). As for Brundage, the last vignette in the book is a one-sentence paragraph, reporting, simply, "Early in 1969, there was a squib in the newspapers announcing that Avery Brundage had arrived safely in Munich to inspect the site of the 1972 games" (119). In retrospect this simple statement is invested with a savage irony that Lipsyte could not have appreciated when he wrote these words in 1970, for it was not until two years later at the 1972 Munich Olympics that a stunned world witnessed an attack on the Israeli team by eight Arab terrorists. Two Israelis were killed immediately and nine others were taken hostage. In a subsequent gunfight, all of the hostages and five of the terrorists were killed.

A second edition of *Assignment Sports* was published in 1984, and it is interesting to note that in it Lipsyte dropped only four of the twenty-four original pieces because they seemed "stale." If the implication is that the remaining twenty are still fresh, the reader will agree. The reason is not only the exemplary quality of the writing itself, but also Lipsyte's original choice of subject and his insights into their real-world context. The game itself—whether it is baseball, boxing, football, or hammer-throwing, whether it is a solo sport or a team endeavor—is transitory. What endures, in sports and in these pieces, are the players and Lipsyte's capacity to show the reader, simply but subtly, their strengths and their weaknesses, their victories and their failures, their very complexity as human beings—all of the things that inspire and challenge the novelist.

In this context it is no surprise that in 1971, a year after *Assignment Sports* was published, Lipsyte, tired of the rigid conventions of the sports column, left the *Times* to pursue a more independent career as a novelist and screenwriter. After four years and eleven months and 544 columns, it was a major move. "I knew I'd miss the quick excitement of deadline journalism," he later reflected, "the tumble-rush after a hot story and the touchdown joy of reading it under my by-line only hours after I had written it. But I wanted more time to think about what I had seen during the past fourteen years, and more space to shape those thoughts into characters and stories."[4]

3. Chasing the Dream

"... an amorphous infrastructure I call ... 'SportsWorld.'"

Lipsyte spent the next eleven years in the basement of his Closter, New Jersey, home working as a free-lance writer, chasing his childhood dream of being a famous novelist and screenwriter. Like most free-lancers, however, he had to find other income-producing opportunities to support himself and his family (a wife and two small children) while establishing his new career. He found these in teaching (at Fairleigh Dickinson, a private university in Teaneck, New Jersey, and at New York University), consulting (for the National Organization for Women and the National Gay Task Force), and, beginning in 1976, doing commentary for National Public Radio. He also served as a senior fellow at Northeastern University's Center for the Study of Sport in Society, setting up programs and teaching.

Despite this hectic schedule, the writing got done. His first adult novel, *Something Going* (written in collaboration with Steve Cady, a fellow sportswriter who covered horse racing for the *New York Times*) was published by Dutton in 1973. In its gritty realism and its insider's look at the behind-the-scenes world of a popular sport, *Something Going* echoes the tone and texture of *The Contender* (the book even features a black groom who, in his affirmation of his manhood, may himself be struggling to become a contender). Its plot, detailing the struggle between the racetrack "haves" (management) and "have-nots" (the grooms, stablehands, and other lower-echelon employees) reaffirms Lipsyte's interest in human issues and his social conscience.

It received mixed reviews, however. While *Newsweek* magazine's Pete Axthelm praised its "hard-edged, thoroughly unsenti-
mental look at a precarious old-world society in the throes of an
upheaval it can't begin to comprehend,"[1] other reviewers were
less generous. They found the plot "melodramatic" and "predictable"[2] and the characters either "routine"[3] or "not too complex"—that is, one-dimensional.[4]

Lipsyte fared only slightly better with his second adult novel, a
solo effort titled *Liberty Two* (1975). A political thriller about an
astronaut who sees the earth "plain" from the vantage of a moon-
walk ("I have seen the purposelessness, the decay, the corruption") and returns to earth to lead a second American revolution,
the novel made "an artistic and political statement that was
important" to Lipsyte. The book received a few good reviews. The
National Review hailed its "good plot, intriguing characters . . .
authentic dialogue . . . and . . . timeliness,"[5] while *Publishers
Weekly* called it "strong stuff—stark, convoluted and frightening-
ly plausible."[6] But most reviewers agreed with Jonathan Yardley,
who, in the *New York Times Book Review*, branded Lipsyte's
"debut as a novelist . . . a distinct disappointment."[7]

A number of reviewers did praise Lipsyte, as a topical novelist,
for having had the insight to discover a subject for his novel of
great intrinsic interest in the wake of the Watergate scandal and
the increasing paranoia it visited on the nation. Indeed, with its
political themes and conspiracy overtones, *Liberty Two*, had it
been published as a young adult novel, would have prefigured
Robert Cormier's 1977 classic *I Am the Cheese*. (Lipsyte is a great
admirer of Cormier, another ex-newspaperman).

In their reviews both R. Z. Sheppard in *Time* magazine and
Yardley in the *New York Times Book Review* praised Lipsyte's
excellence as a journalist (a backhanded compliment, perhaps, for
a fledgling novelist who has left that world behind). Sheppard
said, "Lipsyte, a former sports columnist who contributed some
of the best prose to appear in *The New York Times*, has not lost
his journalist's instincts."[8] For his part Yardley refers to Lipsyte
as "a brilliant young sports writer during his too brief stint as a

New York Times columnist" and praises the "toughmindedness of his sports writing" (Yardley, 36).

SportsWorld

The cool reception to his novels (and the backhanded praise for his earlier sportswriting) may explain why Lipsyte's next adult book was a work of *non*fiction about the world he knew best: *SportsWorld* (1975). Though it incorporates passages—even whole pages—from *Assignment Sports*, this is a much more complex and extended work that expands the earlier book's theme of the social and political context of sports, which has metastasized in this later book into what Lipsyte now thinks of as "a dangerous and grotesque web of ethics and attitudes, an amorphous infrastructure that acts to contain our energies, divert our passions and socialize us for work or war or [economic] depression" (ix).

Though not published as a young adult book, *SportsWorld* is perfectly accessible to young readers and, indeed, says many important things to them about the negative impact that over-commercialization has had on sports and the false value system that "SportsWorld" seeks to impose on American youth (that is, winning is everything, the coach is always right, a test of manhood is playing through pain, and so on).

SportsWorld is beautifully, even artfully written. Here, for example, is Lipsyte observing Kareem Abdul-Jabbar on the basketball court: "For me, his finest moments came when he gracefully rose like a genie from a bottle, the ball resting on his outstretched right palm as if it were on a silver tray" (155). On other occasions, Lipsyte watches an editor "snapping off perfect headlines like chocolate squares" (6) and captures the temper of an era in one sentence: "[Football player] Jim Brown's hard black anger was smashing through fat Sundays" (8).

Lipsyte's look at sports is not only artful but insightful: he describes the post-game scene in a professional football locker room in which the team owners line up against the wall to "gape at the meat. Their meat" (66–67). The "meat," of course, refers to the football players, and it is Lipsyte's way of introducing the issue of the dehumanization of the professional athlete "who can be exchanged for money, goods, services, or another athlete," a theme that will also inform his later young adult novel *The Chief* (1993).

Lipsyte expertly extrapolates from this the idea that "the athlete's role is the traditionally 'female' role. He is selected and rewarded for beauty and performing skills" (67). In other words, the athlete is subjected to the same kind of objectification (that is, dehumanization) that women in our society have traditionally suffered. Lipsyte also understands that sportswriters have colluded in this process: not only by blandly accepting SportsWorld hype and puffery, but "by layering sports with (their own) pseudo-myth and fakelore, by assigning brutish or supernatural identities to athletes, the [Grantland] Rice-ites dehumanized the contests and made objects of the athletes" (172–73). (Lipsyte refers to the followers of the late sportswriter Grantland Rice, who delighted in presenting his accounts of sporting events in mock-heroic style, calling contestants "David and Goliath," for example, and filling his columns with references to Greek mythology and figures of speech borrowed from the battlefield.)

Once started, this process, like an avalanche, is nearly impossible to stop. *SportsWorld* is an invitation to the reader to think about such insights, to challenge the SportsWorld "givens." It is no surprise that Lipsyte's personal heroes are athletes like Harry Edwards, Muhammad Ali, and Jack Scott, renegades all, who have issued their own personal challenges to the system, have countered the sports culture and survived the inevitable controversy, and have succeeded in small and large ways in restoring a human dimension to what has become "a grotesque distortion of sports."

Not surprisingly, *SportsWorld* was greeted with the same degree of controversy that Lipsyte's earlier *Times* columns had excited. The erudite Garry Wills, writing in the *New York Review of Books*, huffed, "If you take Lipsyte's advice and cease to care about professional sports, there is nothing much left to care about in his book except himself; and BobsWorld makes Sports-World seem, by contrast, heaven."[9] Admittedly this is a funny, though rather mean-spirited, assessment, but it seems to be an almost willful misreading of the book, the whole point of which was that Lipsyte does care passionately about sports. What he decries are the meretricious aspects of sports as entertainment. What he would have us do is not "to cease to care about professional sports," as Wills alleges, but, instead, to explore "the possibility that if sports could be separated from SportsWorld, we could take a major step toward liberation from the false values, the stereotypes, the idols of the arena that have burdened us all since childhood" (iv).

Given Lipsyte's passion and the large-as-a-fullback issues he tackles, the tone of *SportsWorld* is often somber. But not unrelievedly so. In fact it is filled with observed moments of humor and with witty writing. For example, when a very young Lipsyte is sent to interview a reluctant Mickey Mantle, the superstar center fielder tries to bean the reporter with a baseball. "I sensed that the interview was over," Lipsyte recalls with deadpan humor (9). Or take this acid description: "[Rocky] Marciano, with his unkempt toupee and his belly bursting through shirts with missing buttons, was not exactly a walking ad for the dignity of ex-kings" (76). (Marciano, an ex-heavyweight champ, had complained to Lipsyte that the new champ, Ali, "demeaned the grandeur of the title.") Lipsyte is also quick to turn his humor, self-deprecatingly, on himself. As Paul D. Zimmerman, in his laudatory *Newsweek* review notes, "He leaves himself room to include a marvelously self-disparaging account of his narcissistic flirtation with tennis."[10]

Whether readers agree or disagree with Lipsyte's opinions in *SportsWorld* is moot. After all, the book's most enduring contribution to the literature of sports is that it invites, challenges, and stimulates the reader to think about the issues he raises. The book is Lipsyte's personal credo and manifesto, a watershed title in his writing career. The points it makes are as timely today as when they were first offered twenty-eight years ago. As Zimmerman concluded in his 1975 review: "Read him and you will never look at a sports event in quite the same way again" (Zimmerman, 122).

Free to Be Muhammad Ali

"My mind, like my notebook, is swollen with Ali."

Perhaps it was inevitable that Lipsyte would write a biography of the heavyweight boxing champion Muhammad Ali, not only because, as Paul D. Zimmerman has pointed out, "Ali [was] Lipsyte's premier subject throughout his journalistic career" (Zimmerman, 122) but also because Lipsyte himself admits that Ali is "far and away the most interesting character in that mythical kingdom I call SportsWorld." Newly assigned to the boxing beat in 1964, Lipsyte first encountered Ali (then still Cassius Clay) at the Fifth Street Gym in Miami Beach, Florida. Waiting impatiently for Clay to show up for his daily workout, Lipsyte was improbably joined by the Beatles—yes, *those* Beatles—who, then on their first American tour and not yet "as famous as Jesus," as John Lennon would put it years later, were not averse to sharing some free publicity with a twenty-two-year-old boxer whose burgeoning public image had been burnished not only by an Olympic gold medal but also by his picture on the cover of *Time* magazine.

Neither Lipsyte nor the Beatles were prepared for the reality behind the image. He recalls their surprise: "Clay burst into the gym, brandishing a cane, and roared, 'Hello there, Beatles.' I gaped and so did the Beatles." Lipsyte continues: "The first beholding of Cassius Clay [was] startling. The exaggeration of the size of SportsWorld heroes . . . has prepared us for disappointment. But Clay was much larger than we had been led to believe. I appreciated Clay that very first day" (*SportsWorld*, 81–83).

To appreciate is not always to understand, however. And Lipsyte admits that while he is often asked what Ali, as he is now known, is *really* like, "To that question I answer: I don't know really. And I'm not sure that he really knows, either."[11] In choosing, some thirteen years later, to write a biography of Muhammad Ali and to grapple with that very question, Lipsyte may have run the risk of receiving the same kind of censure he had received, as a white man, for writing *The Contender*, a novel about another African-American. But this time the reviews were unanimously favorable, hailing Lipsyte's insider's knowledge, his even-handed appraisal of Ali, his thoughtfulness, and his candor.

Lipsyte himself has been more than candid about sports biographies as a genre: he has been blunt in calling them "the junk food of publishing." "They're all too easy to produce," he argues. "You get scissors and a paste pot, raid the newspapers for false biographies of the hero of the moment—and sports writers never were trustworthy in terms of biographical material—and make a book" (Miles, 46). This may seem slightly disingenuous, since a faint scent of the paste pot hovers over *Free to Be*. Certainly moments and scenes from it are borrowed from Lipsyte's earlier writings in *Assignment Sports* and *SportsWorld*, but what separates Lipsyte from those he criticizes is that he is reworking his own material and enhancing it, not simply borrowing someone else's words. The resulting book succeeds splendidly in showing us not only the man but the milieu that was such a powerful influence in the making of the man. As Lipsyte notes in the introduction, "His life touched and was touched by the civil rights movement, the anti–Vietnam War movement, the rise of the gold-plated age of sports, and the television takeover of entertainment and thought" (2).

Lipsyte understands the powerful irony of the circumstances of the young Cassius Clay who, having just won an Olympic gold medal and having praised the United States to an antagonistic Soviet journalist for the advantages of democracy it offers, returns to a hometown (Louisville, Kentucky) where "even with that gold medal on his chest he couldn't eat with white folks. . . . back home he was referred to as 'that Olympic nigger'" (5). There is ironic foreshadowing of Ali's religious conversion (and attendant name change) as well, in Lipsyte's reporting of the beefy congratulations of Kentucky's governor, "who said, 'Boy, I know you proud of that name Cassius Clay. I know you proud to carry that name'" (22).

When, in due course, Clay signs with the Louisville Sporting Group, an investment partnership made up of (white) Louisville millionaires who bankroll his early professional career, he realizes "that they perceived him as a sporting property, like their thoroughbred horses and foreign cars." And yet, amazingly, a black minister publicly admonishes Clay to "be eternally grateful for what those kind Christian millionaires are doing for [your] black soul" (23). (Inevitably the reader is reminded of the mealy-mouthed minister at Aunt Pearl's church in *The Contender*.)

If Lipsyte is bluntly powerful in showing the "routine racial discrimination" that Clay experienced growing up "in a city that has never decided whether it is Northern or Southern" (24), he is more subtle and understated in suggesting the origins of Clay/Ali's adult narcissism, boasting, and self-promotion. The reader may surmise, from Lipsyte's rather sketchy portrait of Ali's father, Cassius Marcellus Clay, Sr.—"a glib, handsome man" with a "flamboyant style"—a hereditary source. The reader may also speculate that the most compelling catalyst for the twelve-year-old Cassius's decision to become a boxer was the prospect of getting on a local television show called *Tomorrow's Champions*. Lipsyte shares a wonderful image of Clay, a week before his first TV appearance, marching around Louisville, "knocking on doors, buttonholing strangers, and interrupting conversations to exclaim: 'I'm Cassius Clay, and I'm having a fight on television. I hope you'll watch me'" (13).

Lipsyte displays a reporter's candor in addressing the larger issue of the "fakelore" that has grown up around Ali's life (and has often been contributed to by the boxer himself), showing the reader, for example, Ali's various versions of the "truth" about the relative importance of his early trainers, the white Joe Martin and the black Fred Stoner. Of another Ali story, Lipsyte says, candidly, "It warrants skepticism. It seems like one of his too-good-to-be-true stories" (20).

Lipsyte helps the reader understand that while some of this truth-embroidering may be nothing more than Ali's showman's desire to tell an ever-better story, more of it may be grounded in the political motivation of a man "whose life is so often displayed as a symbol." As for the rest, well: "Ali, who has heard so many versions of his life, may not always know himself what is authentic and what has been fictionalized" (12). Nevertheless Lipsyte consistently demonstrates that if any person, other than the champ himself, is equipped to sort truth from fiction, it is he. For unlike other writers who must resort to scissors and paste pot, Lipsyte has the advantage of resorting to his own notebook and memory, because he was there, physically present at virtually all of the public *and* private moments that contributed to the making of the man who is arguably the century's greatest boxer and a key figure in the athletic revolution. As Lipsyte observes, "his declaration after winning the championship [his 1964 defeat of Sonny Liston]—'I'm free to be who I want' [hence, Lipsyte's title]—was the single most important statement of the so-called Athletic Revolution in which athletes began to liberate themselves from the phony roles and false values imposed upon them by owners and coaches and journalists and fans" (2).

As Lipsyte compellingly demonstrates in this biography, Ali's personal fight to establish his own authentic identity on his terms was as difficult as any fight he undertook in the ring, and his refusal to compromise his principles, even when it appeared that he would go to jail for them, may be the single most memorable thing about this larger-than-life figure. "Mr. Lipsyte presents a thoughtful, complex portrait of one of America's greatest athletes," one reviewer wrote, adding a telling, one-sentence assessment of Lipsyte's integrity and innovative talent as a sportswriter: "He does so with taste and an honest resolve to delve beyond the usual level of puffery and jock hype, which in his own field makes him almost as unique as Ali."[12]

In terms of subject and theme, *Free to Be* is a natural successor to *Assignment Sports* and *SportsWorld*. In the chronological order of Lipsyte's work, however, it was preceded by his one produced screenplay, *That's the Way of the World* (also known as *Shining Star*). Released in 1975, this dramatic film was an exposé of the record industry. While it largely failed with audiences and critics because of its poor production values, film critic Leonard Maltin generously claims it is saved—"barely"—by its "intriguing look behind the scenes of [the] music business."[13] (A second screenplay, *The Act*, a political satire about how and why

Richard Nixon killed Jimmy Hoffa, was also produced but was undisputedly an artistic failure, closing virtually the day it opened.)

Prior to the publication of *Free to Be*, Lipsyte also worked for thirteen weeks as a scriptwriter for a television program called *Saturday Night with Howard Cosell*, and, for nine months in 1977, he wrote a "cityside" column about people and issues for the *New York Post* (an experience that provided part of the inspiration for his 1982 novel for young adults, *Jock and Jill*). Lipsyte may have had adolescent dreams about being a screenwriter and novelist, but the adult reality of both experiences failed to match the fantasy. Lipsyte found he disliked the enforced collaborative nature of screenwriting and candidly admits that his two adult novels "went nowhere." Obviously by the second half of the seventies he was ready for a new creative challenge, but he was surprised to discover that it would materialize as another young adult novel.

4. The YA Writer Redux

"He tries too hard to teach, as if our heads were drums. . . . "

Lipsyte had always considered himself "a one-shot YA author. My future, I thought, would be in rewriting King Lear, not Kid Lear" ("Listening," 293). Then, one night, as he was writing a magazine article about books that had been important to him as a boy, the phrase "in the prison of my fat" dropped out of his typewriter, and Lipsyte suddenly found himself thinking about his experiences as an overweight teenager. His memories fired his imagination, and, to his surprise, he found himself writing a novel about an overweight fourteen-year-old named Bobby Marks. The publication of this book, *One Fat Summer*, in 1977 marked Lipsyte's return and recommitment to the field of young adult literature.

As previously noted, it was followed by *Free to Be* (1978) and then, in 1981 and 1982, two other novels about Bobby Marks, which chart his further transformation from "The Crisco Kid" to a slim, socially conscious eighteen-year-old standing on the threshold of adulthood. The latter year also saw the publication of *Jock and Jill*, a hybrid novel of sports and social realism.

Though published in the next decade, *Jock and Jill* seems more appropriately to belong to the 1970s, since it thematically re-examines and expands many of the concerns the author first explored in both *SportsWorld* and his 1977 *New York Post* columns. Accordingly it seems logical to examine it here and to defer detailed examination of the Bobby Marks trilogy to the next chapter. For similar reasons Lipsyte's first bout with testicular cancer, which occurred in 1978, will be discussed in the context of his 1992 novel, *The Chemo Kid*.

Jock and Jill

On one level *Jock and Jill* can be read as an exciting, page-turning sports story about how Jack ("Jumpin' Jack") Ryder, a talented, suburban New Jersey high school pitcher, is challenged to re-examine his personal priorities and his commitment to baseball. On another, more sophisticated level, however, the book is a passionate indictment of the abuse of talented youth by ambitious coaches, sports doctors, and naively overenthusiastic parents. On still another level it is an examination of the social awakening of an athlete to the problems of poverty, politics, greed, and corruption, and the efforts of an unconventional grassroots coalition to improve the lives of the impoverished and hopeless in the wasteland of the South Bronx. Finally it is a love story complicated by drug abuse and self-deception. If this sounds like an overly ambitious and potentially confusing agenda for a 153-page young adult novel, it is.

Lipsyte has said that "of course, truth is stranger than fiction. Because fiction has to make sense. The only way we can make sense of our world is by thinking about it in some structured way. Fiction is like a scaffolding you stand on to look at yourself, look at life, and look at the world around you." Unfortunately the reader may be justified in thinking that this particular scaffolding has been too hastily and flimsily constructed to support such a heavy thematic agenda, and so it collapses before all of the truths (that is, real-world problems) it attempts to address can be successfully translated into fictional terms.

On the other hand, Lipsyte is too fine and intelligent a writer to produce a book without some redeeming features. One of these, surely, is the multidimensional character he has created as his protagonist: teenager Jack Ryder. When we first meet Jack, he is walking out to the pitcher's mound for the bottom half of the ninth inning. His prowess as a pitcher has led his team, the Nearmont (New Jersey) Tigers, to within three outs of advancing to the final game of the Metro Area championship, which will be played in Yankee Stadium. What happens next serves to introduce two major elements of the plot: First Jack notices a girl taking photos from a fence-top perch. He can tell immediately that she is not his type at all and wonders, accordingly, why he seems to feel so powerfully attracted to her. Secondly, aware that this is distracting him from his immediate first priority, the game, he demonstrates his strength of character by telling himself to clamp a lid on it and begins throwing his warmup pitches.

The next thing that happens is that Jack realizes that his arm is weakening. What is wrong? His coach, walking out to the mound, provides the answer to the reader with a question: "Elbow hurts, doesn't it?"[1] It is quickly revealed that Jack has a medical problem with his pitching elbow and has been receiving shots from the team doctor to hold the pain at bay. And now the painkiller is wearing off. The coach's reaction introduces another major plot element: instead of removing Jack, who is obviously in pain and in danger of permanently damaging his elbow, the coach simply reminds him that if he can endure his pain through three more outs, the team will be in the championship playoff. In other words, play through the pain, because, in SportsWorld, winning is everything.

Lipsyte has recalled a similar episode from his own youth when, playing softball, he fell and ripped his arm open on a rusty nail. "I was really scared but the coach ran out and looked at it and said it was going to be all right. Then he spat on it. And it *was* all right. . . . I was going through the male myth, being tough and masculine and behaving as I was expected to behave. I was playing hurt. But I know that if anybody ever treated my son like that today, I'd kill him" (Miles, 46).

Jack is also "going through" the male myth, and, seeing his family in the bleachers, he stoically thinks that he must not let them down. Needless to say, *Jack's* father, a true believer in the myth, is not about to kill anybody (although he might have a stroke cheering so lustily for his son). Jack hangs tough, playing through the increasing pain. But when the third batter slams a triple, the coach heads back to the mound. Does he insist now, in the interest of Jack's health, on bringing in a relief pitcher? No. He admits he *can* do that, but "if you can go the distance, you'll have something to be proud of the rest of your life. This is where you find out if you're a man" (6). Jack buys this "philosophy" and resumes pitching. With two outs the batter hits a pop-up and Jack runs to catch it. He does, winning the game, but in the process he accidentally collides with the girl he has noticed earlier, and the lens from her camera smashes into his left eye.

This is not exactly meeting "cute," as Hollywood script writers would put it, but a meeting *has* taken place, and the reader understands that Jack will hear more from this young woman who has captured his attention and that the makings of yet another plot element (a love story) have been established.

In chapter two Lipsyte takes the reader home to meet the family. Unfortunately the parents are essentially one-note characters, attitudes more than fully realized personalities: mom's function is, rather fecklessly, to worry, while Dad is a blowhard and booster who routinely spouts SportsWorld platitudes. Jack's younger brother, Donnie, is mentally retarded, a sweet-natured boy who idolizes his big brother. For a critic Donnie is a troubling character because there is no organic reason growing out of the book's thematic grounding for his mental incapacity. If *Jock and Jill* were real life, we would shrug and say, in effect, "Well, that's life." But fiction is *not* life. As Lipsyte himself has observed, "Fiction has to make sense." The only "sensible" reason the reader can imagine for Donnie's retardation is to reveal another aspect of Jack's character through his interaction (patient and loving) with his unfortunate younger brother. More cynically, Donnie exists as a way for Jack to assess other people's character through *their* reactions to the boy.

On the other hand, there is no question about the viability of a fourth character: Jack's grandmother. She is the sharp-tongued voice of reason speaking in a tone that sounds like "the sharp, uneven little teeth of a ripsaw blade" (21). A retired school secretary, Grandma is a devotee of health magazines and is the only one in the family who can see through the SportsWorld cant to the reality of the long-term problems of playing through pain and the potentially disastrous side effects of painkillers and other sports medicines. When Jack's father blusters that Jack's only physical problem is a strained tendon, "which is being treated," Grandma's tart reply is that "the symptoms are being treated . . . With God knows what long-term side effects" (9).

Just as Spoon was Lipsyte's alter ego in *The Contender*, so is Grandma in *Jock and Jill*. Both adults, though firmly grounded in the reality of the moment, can extrapolate viable futures for the adolescents about whom they clearly care very much. Grandma's concern that Jack's future not be plagued by residual side effects from sports medicines or long-term physical damage derived from playing through pain are reflections of Lipsyte's own concerns and the unfortunate realities of high school and college athletics. In *SportsWorld*, Lipsyte noted that "the so-called gladiator mentality develops in high school, where athletes are often allowed to play hurt by ambitious coaches" (278); and "sports are not necessarily good for you . . . the permanent elbow damage suffered by Little League pitchers has been well documented" (214). In *Harper's* magazine Lipsyte later observed that "the serious drug issues in sports—the abuse of pain-killers and anti-inflammatory medicines, the fact that 'well-meaning' parents and coaches are feeding steroids and other drugs to high school kids—are pretty much ignored."[2]

As Jack's "big game" in Yankee Stadium and its attendant pressures draw nearer, this issue will receive greater attention. But before that can happen, Lipsyte introduces another major issue. The agency for this will be the girl whom Jack has encountered in the first chapter. Following a lazy afternoon spent fishing with Donnie, Jack returns home to find a long black limousine bearing official city plates parked in the driveway. "It was her," Jack thinks (18). And, indeed, it is. Her name is Jillian, and, frustrated by Jack's earlier refusal to take her phone call, she has decided to come to his home to apologize in person for having injured his eye with her camera. Rather improbably the mayor (who is a friend of Jillian's parents) has let her borrow the limo thinking that Jack might sue the city "if we aren't nice to you" (20).

Though we see much more of her than we do of Jack's parents, Jillian is another unsatisfactory character. One senses that she exists not as a person but only as a device to enable the author to introduce thematic issues or problems. For example, feeling the pressure of being cross-examined by Grandma, Jill begins to fidget in her chair and then fishes a box out of her pocket, takes a pill from the box, and swallows it. It develops from this that Jill lives in a halfway house for troubled adolescents in Greenwich Village (Jack thinks of it as "Horror House"), where she is receiving drug therapy for some vaguely defined emotional problems.

The parallel between the two kinds of drug use that Jack and Jill are experiencing is potentially interesting but ultimately seems layered on the narrative by an author who then forces the point in a clumsy exchange between the two characters later in the book. When Jill offers Jack his choice of a green pill or a white pill (one is an amphetamine, the other, a tranquilizer), he loses his temper and shouts that the pills turn her into a zombie. At first Jill can only weakly reply, "They're just little helpers. Prescribed medicine." "It's all the same," Jack shouts. Suddenly (and improbably) Jill rallies and demands, "What about the shots for your elbow?" "That's different," Jack replies. "I don't think so," is Jillian's cool reply (119). The point, of course, is that this is *not* Jill's reply; it's Lipsyte's.

The same failure of fictional technique has already occurred in a scene where Grandma, sounding like an old *Encyclopedia Britannica* classroom film, lectures Dad that "a number of long-term side-effects can be traced to abuses in sports medicine." When Dad tries to defend the integrity of the coach and the team physician, Grandma presses ahead: "Coach Burg wants to win. And what do doctors know? Only what the drug companies tell them. Look at Thalidomide, DES, all these additives." The scene's tone suddenly and unfortunately changes from didactic (which is bad enough) to "Saturday Night Live" sketch comedy (which is even worse) as the now-apoplectic Pop starts to storm off to work and Mom chirpily chimes in, "Don't forget your Maalox" (74–75)—and don't trip over Grandma's pointer and flip chart on your way out, the reader silently adds.

Jack sturdily reassures his grandmother that he understands her concern. And tough-minded Grandma's improbably saccharine response is to touch his cheek and coo, "you've always been such a good person" (75). Of course, Jack *is* a good person. Lipsyte's problem is how to demonstrate this. Once again, he resorts to the deus ex machina device of Jill, who introduces Jack to Hector, a Puerto Rican ex-gang leader who has a social agenda: to turn his gang into a "collective of youth" (43) and clean up the South Bronx. Hector's strategy is to take over tenement buildings from slumlords and clean them up, one building at a time.

It is not an impossible dream and is, in fact, based on Lipsyte's own observation. As a columnist for the *New York Post*, Lipsyte recalls, "I spent most of my time posted in the South Bronx." The region "was being offered up by the media and the government as a symbol of hopelessness in America. But . . . that wasn't the story at all. Gangs were doing sweat equity, kids were getting music lessons, people were trying to get off welfare, get an education, get a job. People were falling in love and building lives, so it wasn't that hopeless."[3]

On the other hand, it was hardly the end of the rainbow, as Lipsyte graphically demonstrates in one of the most powerful and successful scenes in the book, when Hector takes Jack and Jill on a tour of a typical apartment building. Worldly readers might think they are in Beirut, as Lipsyte describes the building rising "out of the rubble of the block like a tombstone in a long-forgotten cemetery" (41). It is even worse inside, where Hector ushers them into a hot, stinking apartment infested with bugs and vermin. The whole chapter has been building powerfully to this point. It reaches a memorable emotional peak in what happens next: they go into the apartment's one ugly and sad bedroom, where Jack is horrified to find two small, silent children tied to a radiator. Hector bitterly explains that the children's single parent, their mother, has gone out to work in a sweatshop, "slaving for a pig who makes big dollars" (46).

Hector is clearly a character who captures Lipsyte's imagination. He is passionate, charismatic, articulate, and street smart enough to be cynical about politicians. When Jill promises to show the pictures she has been taking of the tenement to the mayor so he can see the shocking reality of life in the neighborhood, Hector sneers that he already knows and does not care. So why, only three pages later, should Hector suddenly be gushing, "Oh, man, just fifteen minutes with the Mayor, I'd make him see it, too" (52)?

The answer lies in a moment of epiphany that has occurred between these two scenes, when Hector suddenly recognizes Jack as the pitcher he has observed in action in the first chapter. "I thought you looked real familiar," he chuckles. "Explains everything, why you so cocky and so ignorant. . . . You're a jock. You don't know what's going down in the world" (48–49). Though the casual reader may not immediately recognize the importance of Hector's statement, it introduces what, to Lipsyte, is the most important theme of the book: the emerging role in American society of the athlete with a social conscience or, as he put it recently, "the jock awakened"—the type of athlete who, like Dave Edwards, Jack Scott, and Dave Meggyessy, is the arguable hero of *SportsWorld*, though not, according to Lipsyte, the most immediate inspiration for Jack's "conversion." "The model for that, interestingly," he revealed recently, "was (Doctor) Benjamin Spock, who was a jock, you know. He was a gold medal winner in the 1924 Olympics and became a major anti-war activist. When properly channelled, that kind of 'jockish' dedication is great. Don't quit. Don't stop. Fight."

Earlier Jack has applied this dedication only to winning the game. But now we have the first hints that he might learn to apply it to the game of life, as well. For Jack's conversion to take, however, he must first join Jill in her rather quixotic quest to arrange a meeting between the mayor and Hector (this is the reason Hector must be manipulated by the author to undergo his own conversion and agree to such a meeting). Indeed, when a preliminary meeting of Jack, Jill, and the mayor finally takes place (on the morning of the day of the big game), the man confronts Jack, demanding to know why such a promising athlete would be involved with a political matter.

What ultimately convinces the mayor and Hector to meet— under conditions disagreeable to them both—is the fact that Jack is working to organize this on the very day he is to pitch the most important game of his life. This says a great deal, of course, about sports stereotypes and the fan's perception that the game is the most important thing in the world to the jock. No wonder the jocks themselves buy into this specious belief. The evolution of a real-world perspective is part of the awakening of the jock's social conscience, as we shall see in a moment.

Meanwhile the author manipulates Hector one more time: after five pages of Hector's railing against the mayor, he suddenly says, "You really trust this Mayor, Jack? You really think he's sincere?" "I do," says Jack. Hector's astonishing reply is, "Okay. You know why I'm gonna do it your way, man? Because you the most straight dude I ever met in my life. If I can't trust you, Jack, I never trust nobody" (120). This amazing pledge of trust comes on only the second occasion that the two have met! It almost seems, at this point, that Lipsyte gives up on reality (and credibility) in his urgent desire to make his thematic points.

Having set the stage for the meeting, Lipsyte hustles Jack off to Yankee Stadium for a confrontation with the coach and the team doctor. Both adults are now determined to give Jack extra medication for his elbow before the doctor has even examined it. But Jack remembers that he has promised his grandmother that he will consult the family before agreeing to any more shots, and, reluctantly, the coach agrees but manages to engineer it so that only Jack's father will be present at the consultation. Jack is uneasy about this but thinks, resignedly, "What am I going to say? I want my grandma?" (129). To do so, of course, would be to call his own masculinity into question, an unthinkable alternative in SportsWorld's male-dominated society. Its macho clichés have been established by an earlier scene in which Coach Burg harangues the team by calling them "girls," a despicable practice but, as Lipsyte has elsewhere noted, "coaches use it all the time on their boy players" ("Listening," 291).

The coach has been canny in limiting the family conference to the father, whose reaction is a sadly predictable and explosive defense of the other two adults. In the face of this tirade, Jack finally capitulates and agrees to the shot. This may seem like an act of weakness, but in fact his very insistence on consulting his family and not blindly accepting the dictates of the coach has in itself been a significant act of defiance and symbolizes the changes sweeping over SportsWorld. As the coach self-pityingly sighs to the father, "It's a different time. Ever hear of Jock Lib?" (130).

As his team takes the field, Jack is not the only player to be riding high on medication. Immediately before the game the student manager has distributed amphetamines to all the players after the coach and the doctor have conveniently left the room. This issue of drug abuse would be handled at greater length by Lipsyte in his 1992 novel *The Chemo Kid* (which is also set in Nearmont and which also features Coach Burg, still reacting to his team's drug abuse by looking the other way), but, for the moment, it is interesting to note how similar Jack's reaction to his medication is to the Chemo Kid Fred Bauer's later reaction to his chemotherapy. Fred feels ice dots coursing through his body when, under pressure, his chemo visits super powers on him. Jack, under similar pressure, feels "hot liquid" coursing through *his* body. "[It] was up to his neck and his mind was a laser beam and his arm was a steel cable. . . . He was an engine, a power plant" (139–40).

The medication superpowers him through seven innings of play and an eight-run lead for his team. Lipsyte's reporting of the game is riveting, and his tone is intensely involving as it weds a straightforward, fast-paced narrative style with intense stream-of-consciousness interludes that take us inside Jack's medication-fevered mind. Jack is two innings away from pitching a perfect game when Jillian appears in the stands and shouts that Hector has been arrested. Has the mayor betrayed him?—a provocative possibility that might have given Lipsyte an opportunity to invest his story with politically significant conflict. But no. On the contrary, it turns out that Hector's arrest was a case of mistaken identity. To make it worse, the mayor, when appealed to, claims there is nothing he can do, it being a police matter. This, of course, is nonsense. But it is urgently important to the author that Hector be hauled off to the hoosegow to give Jack a motivation powerful enough for what he will do next. Reality is, thus, once again sacrificed for thematic purpose.

"Hector trusted me," Jack declares. "That's why he's in jail now. Because he trusted me" (142–43). The moment of truth has arrived. Jack must decide what to do. And he does the right thing. Despite the pleadings of the coach (and even of Jill), Jack decides that he does not care about the game—"that's all it is, a game"—and he walks away from it. Fair enough, but unfortunately what he chooses to do next violates the tone and texture of a novel of serious realism, which is what Lipsyte has been writing to this point. It transforms the novel into an action comic book or the script of a B-movie.

With Jill in tow, Jack races to the top of the stadium and hijacks the electronic scoreboard, pushing its operator out of the room and locking the door behind her. His plan is to use the scoreboard to tell everyone in the stadium what has happened to Hector. How can he work a complex piece of electronic equipment he has never seen before? Simple: "It's like a computer keyboard," he tells Jill, "I took Basic Programming this semester, but I missed a lot of classes for practice. I think I can figure this out if I can find the manual" (145–46).

Yeah, right.

Of course he does find the manual; he does send the world a message about the state of the South Bronx and Hector's plight. He does go the distance and, as the stadium security forces tear the door down, flaky Jill realizes that she has gone the distance, too, thanks to Jack's example.

Fade to black.

So Jack gets three months probation. Jill is whisked off to California by her indulgent parents, who are going to check out colleges for her. Dad's not mad—despite the fact that his number one son has thrown away a place in the record books ("It's good to get this kind of craziness out of your system early" [151])—and neither is the coach. Hector is released from jail, and, as Grandma sourly observes, "He got all that publicity [and] they're talking about a TV movie" (151). And, lest the reader think Jack has copped out, here is what the smooth operator is thinking: "She [Jill] won't be in California forever. I won't be in New Jersey forever. Jock and Jill aren't finished climbing hills" (153).

Even Lipsyte admits that "technically it was difficult" to marry a sports story and a serious theme of social awareness. Too difficult to bring off with complete success, perhaps. In a recent discussion of the book he referred to its "undigested qualities," including the politics and Jack's relationship with Hector, as well as his belief that the central theme of the "jock awakened" was "never really worked out properly." He also agrees that certain scenes, including one in which Jack visits a sedated Jill at her halfway house, are too "cartoonish" for an otherwise realistic novel.

Despite these flaws, the author is still fond of the book (and particularly of the characters of Grandma and Donnie) and certainly continues to believe in the importance of social awareness. As he told another, earlier interviewer: "I like characters who are socially aware. . . . I don't see how you can have characters, real characters in YA literature who don't see what's going on. . . . I don't know that at seventeen you have to do something about it but I think at seventeen you can be aware" (Kenny, 287).

Despite its flaws as a novel (and obviously there are many), the book's redeeming quality is that it continues to make its readers aware of their human responsibility "to see what's going on around [them]." Let the last word about this go to the distinguished critic John Leonard, who, like Lipsyte himself, is noted for his social awareness: after praising Lipsyte for what he has to say about the "wretchedness in the South Bronx" and about class antagonism and personal trust, Leonard concludes that while "he tries too hard to teach, as if our heads were drums . . . what he insists that we know is crucial; it implies that most venerable of Buddhist virtues, reciprocity. Which means fairness."[4]

5. *One Fat Summer*
At Last

"I knew that summer I was cutting grass and losing weight that
I would want to write about it."

Teenager Bobby Marks has two strikes against him: he is fat and
he is a summer boy, scorned for the former and resented for the
latter by the year-round residents of Rumson Lake, a resort community somewhere in Upstate New York where Bobby's parents
have purchased a vacation home, a weekend and summer get-
away from the urban stress and mess of New York City. Lipsyte's
1977 novel, *One Fat Summer*, is the award-winning story of
Bobby's self-transformation from a wisecracking, obese adolescent into a wisecracking, slender one. More importantly it is also
the story of how, in the process, the boy finds self-respect, awakening maturity, and the attendant realization that manhood
means more than muscles and a macho mentality.

Lipsyte had always thought that the semiautobiographical *One
Fat Summer* would be his first book. "I knew that summer that I
was cutting grass and losing weight that I would want to write
about it." Circumstances dictated otherwise, and not only did
The Contender beat it to the punch of publication, but for nearly
a decade it appeared that Alfred Brooks's story, not his own,
would be Lipsyte's *only* young adult novel. However, by 1976 the
author was ready for a new challenge. As previously noted, he
had left the security of the *Times* in 1971 to pursue an independent career writing screenplays and novels. However, he recalls,
"I wasn't enjoying writing screenplays because you had to collab-
orate with people, and they were assholes. And then what finally

appeared up there [on the screen] was not what you had in mind in the first place." (This cynical—some would say realistic—attitude about Hollywood is dramatized in his 1993 novel *The Chief*.)

As for his fiction? "My 'old adult' novels went nowhere," he bluntly observes. These are strong motivating factors but, according to Lipsyte, "What really stimulated it [finally writing *One Fat Summer* and returning to the YA lists] was that I was doing a piece for *Mother Jones* magazine about books that affected me as a kid. And I suddenly realized that I had never really dealt with being fat. I had *approached* it a number of times, in a number of different ways, but I never dealt with what it was *really* like. It was too painful. It was a very painful time." Nevertheless when he found himself actually typing the pregnant phrase "in the prison of my fat," he knew he had to write about the experience. "The next day I started writing *One Fat Summer*. And it was all there. Obviously I had been writing it in my head. I lost the weight in 1952 and I started writing about the experience in 1976, so it was like twenty-four years of invisible writing. No book has ever flowed out the way that one did."

Perhaps because the book had such a long gestation period and because it was so personal, *One Fat Summer* has been among his most successful books with readers and especially with critics. It was named both a *New York Times* "Outstanding Book of the Year" and an ALA Best Book for Young Adults the year of its publication and has become a fixture on ALA's retrospective "Best of the Best" lists produced periodically in the years since. It also appears on Alleen Pace Nilsen and Kenneth L. Donelson's master list of the best books published for young adults from 1967 through 1983.

In keeping with its semiautobiographical subject matter, *One Fat Summer*—unlike its predecessor, *The Contender*—is told in the first-person voice of its protagonist. Bobby's voice, like Lipsyte's own, is breezy, irreverent, and, despite the problems that plague his fourteenth summer, quite funny, though usually in a self-deprecating way. The late Norma Klein, herself a groundbreaking young adult writer, has observed of Bobby that "he delights the reader with the engaging urban freshness of his point of view" and that he is "a character out of early [Philip] Roth." (Other reviewers have compared Bobby's voice with early Woody Allen.) In this same context Klein praises Lipsyte as being one of the first young adult writers to create "anything akin to the Jewish novels that have been a mainstay of adult fiction for so long," arguing that "until recently the vast majority of children's book writers were non-Jewish and their books had rural, homespun, wholesome themes."[1]

In telling his story, Bobby gets right to the point. "I always hated summertime," he begins, "when people take off their clothes. In winter you can hide yourself. . . . But in the summertime they can see your thick legs and your wobbly backside and your big belly and your soft arms. And they laugh." How fat is Bobby? "I weighed more than 200 pounds on July 4th. I don't know exactly how much more because I jumped off the bathroom scale when the number 200 rolled up."[2] How fat was Lipsyte at fourteen? He ruefully admits he does not know his exact weight, since—like Bobby—he "always jumped off the bathroom scale as the mocking red arrow began to fly past 199, my last known address in the prison of fat" ("Prisoner," 32).

Precise numbers are secondary, however. Of primary importance is what Bobby's size has done to his life. When we first encounter him, he is at the Rumson Lake Community Association Carnival on the Fourth of July—but only because it is so unseasonably cool that he is able to wear a long-sleeved shirt outside of his pants. Despite this camouflage, which he often resorts to, he has no sooner arrived at the carnival than a local tough yells one of the most famous lines from the book: "Hey, it's the Crisco Kid" (2). When one of the others asks, as if it were a carefully rehearsed comedy routine, why his friend has called Bobby that, the unflattering answer is, "because he's fat in the can" (2).

Bobby has heard this kind of abuse often enough to understand that the best way to deal with it is to pretend he has *not* heard it. His best and perhaps only friend, Joanie Miller, also understands the wisdom of this and with equally good reason, for her large and unsightly nose is as much an object of abuse as Bobby's obesity.

These two outsiders have been friends and mutual confidants since they were three. Bobby's rueful thought, "We not only grew up together, we grew *out* together" (4), is typical of the flip, self-deprecating humor he brings to his attitude. That is one joke he has *not* shared with his friend, though. A measure of their mutual pain is the fact that these two confidants freely talk about everything in the world except their physical problems, as if a conspiracy of silence about them will make them disappear.

Bobby feels sorry for Joanie, for he is convinced that while his fat will someday vanish, her nose will be a permanent fixture. It will not be, and in fact, though Bobby does not yet know it, his friend has already secretly chosen to act on her problem by undergoing cosmetic surgery. This is in sharp contrast to Bobby, for the reader understands that he is prepared to do nothing about *his* problem except to daydream about its going away. Joanie's decision, and the absence it will impose, becomes the de facto catalyst for change in Bobby's life, however, for it removes the excuse he had planned to use to frustrate his strong-willed father's summer plans for him; that is, he and Joanie had planned to do a special project for extra school credit that summer. Without that project, Mr. Marks will insist that Bobby become a junior counselor at a local day camp—an unacceptable option to him, since it means donning a swimming suit and exposing himself to the laughter of the small children who would be in his charge.

A measure of Bobby's self-loathing and disgust with his body is that he cannot bring himself to tell even Joanie the truth about this. Instead he lamely explains his aversion to the job by claiming that he hates little kids. Joanie demonstrates *her* toughness and capacity for action in the face of adversity by insisting that Bobby look for alternative work. It is she who first suggests a job mowing lawns. Bobby weakly equivocates, and when Joanie suggests finding appropriate job openings posted on the bulletin board near the snack bar, he counters by suggesting that they find something to eat first. When Joanie is adamant, Bobby finally calls a prospective employer and, to his surprise, is offered a job interview the next day.

As this is unfolding, Lipsyte has introduced his readers to two other major characters: the book's arguable hero, Pete Marino, and its inarguable villain, Willie Rumson. A sophomore in college, Pete is a lifeguard at his family's beach club on the lake. His typical garb, a skimpy bathing suit and a Saint Christopher medal, reveals the kind of lean, muscular body Bobby wistfully wishes *he* had. Despite his good looks and his obvious vanity about them, the lifeguard nevertheless becomes a hero in Bobby's eyes when he stands up for Bobby and Joanie against Rumson, a local "punk" who, despite his dishonorable discharge from the Marine Corps, still parades about in combat boots and fatigue hat and tries to prove his manhood by leading his gang in insulting the defenseless Bobby and Joanie.

It is Bobby's turn to hotly defend Pete when his older sister Michelle criticizes the lifeguard for his vanity. The mildly acerbic exchange that follows not only establishes the nature of Bobby and Michelle's bantering, younger brother/older sister relationship, it also leads to an important revelation about Bobby. One of the more vexing challenges to a writer who has chosen the first-person voice is how to reveal aspects of the protagonist's character. Lipsyte chooses, artfully, to have other characters introduce certain necessary information. For example Joanie, through her comments, has already established that Bobby is highly intelligent. Now she sighs, "I guess you will be a writer when you grow up. . . . You're such a liar already" (19).

This sounds like an exasperated older sister's exaggeration, but in fact Bobby is something of a liar; he will lie about his age and his work experience, for example, to get the lawn-mowing job. But more often he simply exaggerates; he embellishes the truth, like many another would-be writer, to make a better story. In telling Michelle about Pete's intervention with Rumson, for example, Bobby admits to the reader that he has made "a few" changes in the story.

Bobby's ambition to be a writer is a natural one for an intelligent, sensitive boy whose size has made him an unhappy outsider and enforced observer of the more active and world-engaging lives around him. His ambition will provide a leitmotif of all three of the books about his summers on Rumson Lake, while his running commentary about his would-be career not only will give the reader insight into Lipsyte's own adolescent ambitions and imaginings but will add believable dimensionality to Bobby's character.

While as a person Bobby is a bit of a liar (or embellisher), as a narrator he is a reliable (though colorful) purveyor of the truth of his own circumstances, and he is candid about reporting things that are unflattering to him. If the substance of what Bobby shares is believable, so is his narrative voice. Given the demonstrated facts that he is intelligent and, as a would-be writer, sensitive to language, the reader accepts the possibility that a four-teen-year-old would sound like Bobby and, more importantly, that Bobby's voice is authentically his own, not Lipsyte's. Stylistically Bobby's narrative employs simple, declarative sentences and large amounts of dialogue enlivened by colloquial language. In the whole of the first chapter there are only two similes (Pete has "big white teeth like Chicklets" and looks "like a movie star") and one metaphor, "cannonball muscles" (which also describes Pete; 19–20).

Once it is established that Bobby is interested in becoming a writer, his voice assumes, in chapter two, a more authorial tone and texture. En route to Dr. Kahn's estate for his job interview, Bobby uses a simile to describe his first glimpse of the lawn: "it looked like a velvet sea." The simile effectively establishes the vastness of the lawn and invites metaphorical extension in the description of the house as "a proud clipper ship" and of the owner, Dr. Kahn, who is standing on the porch, as "the captain on the bridge of the ship" (21).

Beyond being equated with the role of captain, Dr. Kahn is memorably described: his eyes are "like shotgun barrels" and his mouth looks like "a slit for old razor blades" (22). True to his description, the man is metallically cold, and his words are cutting. "You are extremely fat for seventeen," he tells Bobby, who has, of course, lied about his age (24). A self-important martinet, he speaks of himself in the third person and tends to talk not in sentences but in pronouncements. For example, Dr. Kahn pronounces himself pleased with Bobby's "enterprise" in walking to work, though this has taken a physical toll on the boy. In describing it, Bobby shows his fondness for using overstatement for dramatic effect: "My stomach [was] boiling. My face was on fire" (21). Such hyperbole will be a hallmark of Bobby's style in all three of the novels about him.

Dr. Kahn's house sits atop a long hill (it typically takes Bobby nine minutes to climb to the top), and his arduous ascent each day inevitably evokes Alfred Brooks's similar climb up the stairs to Donatelli's gym. Determination serves Bobby as well as it did Alfred, for he gets the job. His elation is tempered, however, by another encounter with Willie Rumson on the way home. Rumson threatens and insults him once again, underscoring his intense dislike not only of Bobby but of all summer residents.

Bobby's next confrontation is not with a local but with his own father who, at the breakfast table the next day, demands to know when his son will make a decision about taking the summer job as a camp counselor. Otherwise, Mr. Marks is convinced, Bobby will do nothing all summer except mope around the house, feeding his misery. The boy's appetite has been a longstanding source of friction between him and his father, who is not only as thin as Bobby is fat but is also as muscular and fit as Pete Marino.

Bobby has also established in the first chapter that his father does not have much confidence in him. This is reinforced now by Mr. Marks's immediate and intemperate rejection of Bobby's tentative, trial-balloon suggestion that he find his own job. Instead of countering the father's outburst with a triumphant announcement that he already *has* secured a job, Bobby instead decides to keep this fact a secret.

This decision becomes the first of what will be a number of deceptions he and the other members of his family will practice that summer. Indeed, in a later chapter Bobby will muse that if he ever writes about his experiences and those of his family that vacation season, he will title it *The Summer of the Secrets*. For the moment Bobby justifies his decision by thinking that even if his father did let him take the job, he would make such an issue of safety precautions that Dr. Kahn would probably fire him, and then everybody would feel sorry for him, thinking that "poor Bobby" had once again been cut from the team.

In an interview four years after the publication of *One Fat Summer*, Lipsyte mused about such "cuts": "The boys now begin a series of qualifications for the rest of their lives, which are called cuts. Somewhere along the line, most boys will get cut. They'll be deemed unworthy boys, and they'll see themselves as inferior because they weren't chosen; they didn't make the team. At a time when they needed it, they didn't get the approval that mattered."[3] In a sense, Bobby is a victim of this same system, not getting the approval *he* needs, either from his father or from his peers. Nevertheless, though Bobby does not yet understand it, Mr. Marks has some justification for his opinions. A few pages later, on Bobby's first day at work, he cannot wait to get his hands on Dr. Kahn's tools, explaining to his readers that his father would never let him use garden tools at home because he thought "I would break them or leave them out in the rain" (37). Bobby is especially excited when Dr. Kahn points out the power mower he will use, explaining disingenuously that his family has only a hand-mower that is rusty because he has left it out in the rain. Bobby may not see the irony of this, but it is not lost on the reader, who wonders what else Bobby has done to undermine his father's confidence in him.

The chapter concludes with Bobby's resolutely setting off for his first day at his new job, dressed in too-tight dungarees and still thinking resentfully of his father's earlier lecture. As he begins the long walk around the lake to his new job, his mood lightens, though, and his cheerful interior monologue about what he sees along the way helps to establish the Rumson Lake setting, to embellish his writer's ambitions, and to offer further background information about Pete Marino and his family.

Waving to a passing truck driver, Bobby wistfully thinks that he might also someday drive a truck. (In fact, in a subsequent novel, *The Summerboy*, he will do just that.) In his adolescent fantasies, truck drivers lead lives of stirring adventure, and he recalls a story about a former laundry truck driver whose act of heroism once made him a local hero. This memory serves two purposes: it cleverly foreshadows a later encounter Bobby will have with the legendary driver's son, and it reinforces, for the reader, Bobby's nascent ambition to become a writer, as he imagines that this epsiode would make a good short story for *The Saturday Evening Post.*

These musings carry Bobby and the reader to the Kahn estate's entrance. Bobby checks his watch and, discovering that it is 8:47, thinks it is probably later than that, since his watch runs slowly because of his low basal metabolism, one of the reasons, he likes self-indulgently to believe, that he gains weight so easily. His father and sister, of course, have high basal metabolisms, and Bobby is self-pityingly convinced that that is the reason the two do not understand his weight problem. In fact, the reader suspects, they do, only too well. In chapter one, for example, Bobby has recorded that his sister has caught him eating five hot dogs, and at the breakfast table earlier that morning, his mother has had to defend him against his father's criticism of his overindulgence. Bobby is grateful to his mother, but the careful reader may understand that her indulgent sympathy is part of the real reason that Bobby is so heavy. But this revolutionary notion has not occurred to Bobby himself, who sees only an ally in his mother and an unremitting antagonist in his father, who, Bobby suspects, is ashamed of having a fat son.

What Bobby wants to be, of course, is his own person, thin *or* fat. Accordingly when he actually begins mowing Dr. Kahn's lawn later that morning, he is elated by the thought that he has gotten a job all by himself without any adult intercession. If Bobby, like Lipsyte at his age, is a prisoner in his own fat, in his imagination he is free and empowered. He creates, as we see in this chapter, heroic alter egos for himself—first in a song he makes up about himself as "Big Bob Marks" and then in a fantasy inspired by John Wayne movies. He is suddenly Captain Marks of the U.S. Cavalry, riding out to rescue the colonel's daughter from a band of renegades led by "Chief Willie Ratface." Unfortunately this pleasant reverie reminds him of a real-life memory. When he was a little boy, his grandparents had sent him a child-size U.S. Cavalry uniform. But it did not fit, because Bobby was too fat to wear it.

This unhappy memory bursts his bubble of elation, and the mood of fantasy-induced euphoria vanishes, replaced by physical pain that is equally exaggerated. He suddenly hurts all over; his sweat becomes acid and the job, torture. Like Alfred Brooks in *The Contender*, he is tempted to quit. Motivation meets opportunity when Bobby sees Dr. Kahn drive away, leaving him alone for the first time that day. There is nothing now to keep him from leaving and going home, but suddenly he once again becomes Captain Marks, who urgently insists that he stay on the job. Bobby—and his story—enter a dreamlike state until Dr. Kahn returns and abruptly restores them both to reality. He assesses Bobby's work and pronounces it a "disgrace," angrily adding that Bobby will have to do it all over again the next day.

Trying to stifle his tears, an exhausted and dispirited Bobby stumbles down to the county road and struggles to Marino's Beach Club and Snack Bar, where he is given water and salt tablets. Pete mistakenly thinks that Bobby, as a summer resident, has been mugged by the Rumson gang. He explains that the lake and all of its surrounding land had once belonged to the Rumsons, who subsequently lost it through financial mismanagement. Rather than accept responsibility, however, they blame summer visitors for their own failure (in somewhat the same way that Bobby blames his basal metabolism for his obesity).

Pete then insists on driving Bobby home in his truck, not out of any particular concern for the younger boy but because it will give him a chance to see Michelle. Bobby, who has probably suffered a mild heatstroke, manages to stagger into the house before fainting. Significantly his last thought is that he has missed lunch, and this triggers an elaborate dream in which he is melting. Although this foreshadows Bobby's ultimate transformation, not from melting but from the hard physical labor of maintaining Dr. Kahn's vast lawn, slenderness remains, for the moment, only wishful dreaming.

The next morning's reality is that he not only is still fat but has blisters and universally aching muscles. Nevertheless, to his credit, he stubbornly returns to Dr. Kahn's and resumes mowing the lawn. At day's end, Dr. Kahn, though loudly dissatisfied with

Bobby's job performance, "magnanimously" offers to let him keep working, but on a trial basis and for half the promised wage. Bobby mumbles his agreement and for the second consecutive day stumbles away in tears. Cry though he might, Bobby has begun taking the first slow, painful steps toward establishing his own identity. But, like many adolescents, he still confuses his body, his physical appearance, with his personal identity, with who he is.

In chapter eight we are reminded of how very unhappy Bobby is with that physical self. Arriving home from work he sits in a backyard swing, catching glimpses of distant swimmers and envying their easy comfort with their bodies. On the rare occasions when Bobby actually goes swimming, he tells us, he tries to stay underwater as long as possible so people will not see his body. In the process he has become a powerful underwater swimmer, a fact that will prove significant to the book's denouement. It will also add another character to Bobby's imagined repertory company of heroic alter egos: Commander Marks, leader of an underwater demolition crew.

Meanwhile he reflects on the pleasures of mindlessly swinging and imagining himself somewhere else as anybody else. Anybody other than his fat, self-loathing self, the reader understands. Indeed Bobby recalls having once imagined himself invisible, a common enough preadolescent fantasy, but one that is singularly appropriate for a boy who, like Bobby, hates his body. The fantasy was spoiled for him when he shared it with the more analytical Joanie, who innocently asked if he would have to remove his clothes to be invisible. The prospect of accidentally turning visible when stark naked and being seen by everybody is so terrible to Bobby that he has never again returned to the daydream.

Thinking of Joanie, Bobby also realizes that he is relieved by her absence. Were she present, she would force him to stand up for his rights against the intimidating Dr. Kahn. "Are you a man or a rug," he imagines her asking and significantly, the only response he can imagine is to jokingly throw himself on the floor and pretend to be a bearskin rug (72–73). To Bobby a challenge has always been something to deflect with humor, not something to deal with.

But, of course, this is not a joke. Bobby understands that Dr. Kahn *is* taking advantage of him, and the reader realizes that when Bobby, thinking about the situation, finds himself becoming angry with the absent Joanie, he is really getting angry with himself for his weakness. His reaction to this unflattering realization is telling: he goes into the house and fixes himself a sandwich. What happens next is equally telling: finding himself with an unexpected opportunity to tell his mother about his new job, Bobby chooses to lie instead, duplicitously telling her that he is working for Pete Marino at the beach club.

Though not overtly stated, it is understandable why, at this stage in his development, Bobby would resort to lies: telling the naked truth would be akin to taking his clothes off in public. But there is more to it than that. He is still struggling to establish his own identity in the face of what, the reader will understand, is continuing parental overprotection. Indeed, Bobby is probably justified in thinking that his mother, like his father, would intrude her concerns on his lawn-mowing job and spoil it for him.

Clearly neither parent has ever permitted Bobby to try things on his own, to test his limits, to make mistakes and to learn from them, which is all the more reason why his triumph of earlier that same day is so significant. For "at exactly 2:17 P.M. I beat Dr. Kahn's lawn. I left that chlorophyll monster chopped to size" (80). Despite all of his earlier reversals, Bobby has persisted—and triumphed. It is a giant first step on the road to self-transformation. And it is underscored by the fact that he later rejects the temptation to reward himself with a frosted malt. Finally having a valid reason to be happy with himself acts as a natural curb on his appetite. A giant step, indeed.

But there will be other steps ahead. Later that week Bobby encounters two more antagonists: Willie Rumson's cousins, the Smith brothers, sons of the heroic truck driver who now operates a landscaping service that Dr. Kahn employs once a week. One of the two brothers, Jim, becomes the chief antagonist, first insulting Bobby, whom he dislikes for "taking" Willie's job from him (Willie had mowed Dr. Kahn's lawn the summer before), and then trapping him on the roof of the pool house by removing Bobby's ladder.

That evening Rumson and the Smiths stop Bobby as he is walking home and try to intimidate him into giving up his job. To everyone's surprise, Bobby refuses to be intimidated. Willie's threat of physical violence is very real, however, and Bobby is saved from injury only by the timely arrival of a local policeman. While the reader will think Bobby has acquitted himself well, for him it is a hollow victory. The policeman turns out to be Willie's uncle, who naturally blames Bobby for the altercation but lets him off with a warning and a boot in the backside. Jogging home, Bobby hears laughter erupt behind him and glumly assumes he is its object. Still depressed when he arrives home, he seeks refuge in sleep and then feels guilty about that, as well.

If Bobby is being too hard on himself for once, it is nevertheless true that he is at least not awake to some of the changes that have been plaguing the rest of his family while he has been preoccupied with his own problems. It is becoming obvious to the reader that Bobby's parents are quarreling and their marriage may be in jeopardy. Meanwhile Michelle has begun dating Pete, and since Mrs. Marks disapproves, Bobby will be drawn into more deception by his sister, who is determined to continue her relationship.

For the moment, however, he is unaware of all this, knowing only that because his father is staying at their New York City apartment, he will enjoy a quiet weekend. When Mr. Marks is around, he is not only loudly impatient with his wife's pampering of Bobby, he is also hyperkinetic, driven to fill the minutes of every day with things to do, things that will involve the whole family. By Sunday Bobby is surprised to realize he misses his father's active presence. He does not miss Mr. Marks's vigilant supervision of his eating habits, however. And yet, while he has the luxury of being self-indulgent in his father's absence, he is surprised at his lack of appetite. Of course, he does have some peanut butter sandwiches and several dishes of ice cream, but "that was more for taste than hunger" (103). Bobby's invocation of his two favorite dishes leads to a very funny, two-page meditation on the perils of eating these two foods too fast: the "peanut butter strangle" and the "ice cream headache."

Bobby may view food as a security blanket, eating when he is depressed or afraid, but there is no question that he simply enjoys the taste of food, too, and often treats it as a reward, an idea that has been instilled in him by his doting mother. By Sunday afternoon, however, Bobby's mother has also departed, and she is not due to return until Tuesday. Since Michelle is spending all of her nonworking hours with Pete Marino, Bobby is left alone at the start of a new week for the first time that summer. Monday starts auspiciously: Bobby surprises Dr. Kahn, and himself, by cutting nearly half the lawn in one day. Then there is further evidence that Bobby's body is changing: his hands are getting calloused, and, though he fixes himself a large dinner that evening, he only eats half of it and goes for a walk instead of finishing the food.

Lipsyte now begins building quietly to one of the most dramatic moments in the book. This is presaged by Bobby's noticing (symbolic) storm clouds covering the sun. Though he knows he should probably head for home, he is enjoying the walk and is reluctant to return to the still-empty house. So he continues on to a little grocery store, where a conversation with the owner reveals the man's anti-black bigotry. Bobby leaves quickly but then berates himself for not starting an argument with the man. He realizes that his father would have done so and wonders what Pete, whose father is a bigot like the grocer, would have said in his situation. The more he thinks, the more disgusted he becomes with himself.

At this crucial moment a car pulls up on the lonely road and, inevitably, it is Willie Rumson who jumps out, spewing the usual insults and threats. Bobby's automatic reply shocks them both: "Take a hike, Rummie" (117). (Though Bobby does not recall it, his hero Pete Marino had used these exact words earlier when Willie was hectoring Bobby and Joanie.) When Willie turns back to his car, Bobby is elated at having called a bully's bluff. But his elation is short-lived, for Rumson is simply summoning his gang from the car: two girls and three boys, one of whom is Jim Smith.

Willie snaps his fingers, and the dangerous reality of Bobby's situation is underscored by two of the boys grabbing his arms.

This is reinforced when Bobby manages to kick Willie in self-defense, and the local threatens to kill him. As his cronies try to dissuade him from this radical action, Willie loses control and, in a vicious coda to the scene in the grocery store, screams *his* prejudices about "fat faggots, smartass Jews and Wops" (120).

Willie's friends are clearly alarmed by his uncontrollable rage and the accompanying threats to kill Bobby. It is one of the girls who quick-wittedly comes up with an idea that will save Bobby's life, but that will be so humilating to him that he would almost prefer the oblivion of death. "Strip him naked," she urges Willie, "and leave him on the road" (122). This appalling prospect gives Bobby the sudden surge of strength he needs to break free. But to no avail. He is quickly recaptured and pushed into the car and blindfolded.

At first Bobby is relieved that he will not be killed and imagines that he will simply be dumped somewhere on a country road and left to a solitary, footsore walk home. But Willie has other plans. He and his friends force Bobby into a boat and row him out to an island in the middle of Rumson Lake. There Rumson and his friends leap on him, and though Bobby desperately fights back, they are too many to resist. Tearing his clothes off, they leave him, alone and naked on the island. As the night explodes with thunder and lightning, Bobby hears their laughter echo and re-echo across the lake. For Bobby, his worst nightmare has been cruelly realized. The invisible boy has become visible. People have seen his body, naked, without even the skimpy covering of a swimming suit. And they have laughed. And laughed. . . .

As chapter twelve begins, Bobby is now convinced that he is going to die. And the reader understands that at that moment, he would welcome it. He sinks to the ground, hoping that no one will ever find his body and know his shame. His narrative turns into a stream-of-consciousness parade of self-pity and self-loathing. As the rising water reaches his shoulders and covers his back, Bobby's self-hatred reaches its apotheosis: "Always making up stories about heroes because you're nothing yourself" (130).

At this desperate moment, Bobby hears a voice commanding him to stand up. He looks around but sees no one in the darkness. He hears the voice again as lightning floods the island with light, but once again he sees no one. The water continues to rise, and Bobby thinks how easy it would be to give up, to let himself drown there in the mud. But the voice is relentless in its refusal to let him be defeated. "YOU'RE NOT GONNA LET THOSE BASTARDS KILL YOU" (131).

Suddenly Bobby recognizes the voice: it is his own. He has become a one-man U.S. Cavalry, riding to his own rescue. The heroes he has imagined are personifications of the personal heroism that has been growing inside him and now, nurtured by his triumphs over the lawn and his defiance of Willie Rumson, suddenly blossoms. The reader silently cheers this beautifully realized moment as Bobby says, simply, "I stood up" (132).

The rest is easy. Bobby finds shelter for the night in an old cabin and makeshift clothing in a filthy old sheet he finds there. The next morning Jim Smith shows up with Bobby's real clothes and rows him back to the shore. His appearance is not an externally imposed plot convenience or a manifestation of some unbelievable change of heart about Bobby. On the contrary, Smith callously explains that he does not care about Bobby; it is Willie he wants to spare from further problems, should Bobby die of exposure.

Returning home and finding the house empty, Bobby showers and has breakfast. Deciding to go to work early, he meets Michelle coming up the hill. Her night, it turns out, has been almost as bad as his: Pete's truck has been stuck in the mud with a flat, and they have spent the stormy night outside. When she anxiously asks if their mother has called, Bobby reassures her that he has provided an alibi. When she thanks him, he sings, "Any time." And then he evidences that his epiphanic experience on the island has changed not only the way he thinks of himself but the way he thinks of other people, as well. Watching his sister laugh in relief, he thinks how pretty she is. And then he skips down the hill, adding that he might have trotted all the way to Dr. Kahn's if he had not thought he might need his strength later on, for "you never know what's going to happen on Rumson Lake" (137).

Theoretically this could have been the end of the book. For Bobby has now demonstrated growth and change; he has shown his independence in getting a job and his perseverance in keeping it; he has conquered the lawn and acquitted himself bravely in encounters with the Smiths and Willie Rumson, and his story has reached emotional catharsis in the transforming night on the island. But as Lipsyte will artfully demonstrate, there are even more significant transformative experiences to come, for both Bobby and others. And in revealing them, the author will build to another emotional peak even more dramatic than the first.

6. More Marks

"Something had happened to me and it wasn't all bad, not at all."

Bobby's transformative experience on the island will serve as the catalyst for a series of changes that will continue to touch not only his own life but the lives of his friends and family, as well. Of all these the most problematic are those impacting his family and his parents' relationship.

At the end of the week following Bobby's adventure, Mr. Marks finally returns from the city for a weekend with his family. He is uncharacteristically quiet, though, more like a houseguest than a family member. Determined to find out what is happening, Bobby hides behind a door and shamelessly eavesdrops on his parents' postdinner conversation, learning thereby that the tension that is troubling their marriage derives from Mr. Marks's disapproval of his wife's plans to continue her education and, ultimately, find employment as a teacher. On the one hand we can easily understand that Mrs. Marks is going about the business of transforming herself, just as Bobby is, and we can appreciate the apposite literary parallel that Lipsyte establishes. But on the other hand her husband's resistance is less easily understood, especially since he has, according to Bobby, been proud of her earlier volunteer work as a teacher in Harlem. And so when he now asserts that her plans are not fair to their children, the reader will sense that this is surely a specious argument. It is more likely that he does not think it is fair to *him*.

Indeed, he may be jealous of his wife's initiative, since, in the conversation Bobby overhears, it is revealed that he is unhappy in his own job and has always wanted to do something else, just as his wife is now proposing to do. To further frustrate Mr. Marks, he has at hand his own opportunity to transform himself in a job offer from Joanie's wealthy father, but he is too concerned about the lack of security this change would impose on him and his family to take the plunge. This behavior is consistent with what Bobby has earlier told us of his father: that he is very security-oriented, highly organized, and always anxious to control every situation. This is one situation he cannot control, however, for change is fraught with imponderables and risk. There is the risk that his wife's taking a job will change the nature of their relationship; there is the risk that it will change the nature of the family's relationships; most importantly there is the risk it may even change the person his wife is.

These are very adult considerations, and in this one instance the reader may not be well served by having a first-person narrator who can only report what he observes, since, at fourteen, he does not have the experience of life or the emotional maturity to analyze it. One thing, however, is obvious: the parents are not able to resolve their difficulties through communication. Every time they try, reason is quickly transformed into argument, which turns into uneasy silence. Mrs. Marks retreats into her books, while Mr. Marks keeps himself frenetically busy with now solitary pursuits.

Given this paradigm, it is no surprise that the members of the Marks family keep so many secrets and practice so many deceptions! Recognizing this and the changes that are transforming his family, Bobby poignantly laments that the one thing he misses is the opportunity to be honest with another person. So he is glad when Joanie calls long distance to announce she is finally returning to the lake, though she still teasingly refuses to tell him her secret. Since by now even the most obtuse reader will have guessed that she has had cosmetic surgery, Bobby's astonishment when he finally sees her seems a bit overdone. Even more surprising to the reader is Bobby's immediate reproach: "You never told me. . . . I mean such a big thing, and we talked about everything else" (160). Apparently Bobby has forgotten that he has earlier told the reader that he and Joanie talked about everything *except* their physical problems. Nevertheless Joanie's lack of candor helps explain why Bobby suddenly feels like a stranger. Since Joanie has always been his best, and perhaps his only, friend, his reaction is particularly poignant: he gobbles a bowl of ice cream to summon the one "friend" he can always count on: "my old ice cream headache pal" (161).

In the days that follow, it becomes increasingly apparent that Joanie's operation has changed more than her physical appearance. Bobby has lost a confidante, and his frustrated inability to communicate with Joanie echoes the problems his parents are encountering with their own failure to communicate. Like Bobby's mother, Joanie is now absorbed with her own concerns. The level of her self-absorption may be measured by the fact that she does not even notice the physical change in Bobby.

Interestingly the first person to do so is the physically perfect Pete Marino who, to Bobby's considerable surprise, one day asks if he has lost weight. Such a revolutionary idea has not even occurred to Bobby, but, thinking about it, he now acknowledges that his pants do feel looser. It is symbolically important that this exterior change, noticed now for the first time, should have been preceded by the even more important interior change Bobby experienced during his nightmare night on the island. This is underscored by Marino's teasing suggestion that the more slender Bobby will probably start doing fancy dives off the high board, the ultimate test of manhood in the lifeguard's eyes. "You don't have to do that to be a real man," Bobby replies (170).

Although this remark is offered without fanfare or comment, it marks another turning point in the book and a giant step toward Bobby's own transformation not only from fat to thin but also from boy to man-in-the-making, from adolescent uncertainty to adult maturity. From this moment the meaning of manhood will emerge as another major theme of the book. Bobby's true test of manhood is still to come. But for the moment the reader will share his elation at this first manifestation of his physical transformation and rejoice as he races home to weigh himself—and for the first time does not have to bail out, since the needle peaks at a respectable 195 and then rolls back to 187. The reader will join

Bobby in grinning at himself in the mirror and echo his ecstatic thought, "Lookin' good, big fella" (171).

Further evidence of Bobby's progress is supplied less than a page later, when Jim Smith tells him that Willie is back in town, threatening, now, to break Bobby's kneecaps unless he quits his job. Neither alternative is attractive, and Bobby understandably spends the rest of the day agonizing and rationalizing so that, by quitting time, he has resigned himself to quitting permanently. But when he actually approaches Dr. Kahn to resign, he realizes that he does not want to quit the job after all. Turning a nice mental phrase, he stubbornly thinks he is not a yo-yo for Smith and Rumson to jerk up and down.

Bobby has taken yet another important step toward his self-transformation: he has changed the way he thinks about himself. And that gives him the courage to keep his job—and even to remind Dr. Kahn that he owes him a dollar for each of the previous two weeks (ironically the doctor of mathematics has been shortchanging him). Bobby has not turned into Superboy, however; he is still a fourteen-year-old kid who is taking a big risk, and he is, frankly, frightened. But Bobby would not be the Bobby the reader has come to know if he did not manage to see this in literary terms: he reflects that being frightened is a good experience for a would-be writer.

From this observation it is a logical step for Bobby to think of Richard Connell's famous short story "The Most Dangerous Game," a staple of textbook anthologies in the fifties. Bobby casts himself as the hero of the story and Willie as the villain, finding comfort in the recollection that the hero of the story bests the villain in hand-to-hand combat. With this thought Lipsyte cleverly foreshadows the rapidly impending climax of Bobby's own story, but neither Bobby nor the reader yet realizes this. Before that can happen, another week will pass in which Bobby must first do figurative hand-to-hand combat with other problems.

Joanie will finally recognize that Bobby has lost weight, but this encounter, like all of their recent meetings, will end in a quarrel, and Bobby, returning home in frustration, goes immediately to his old friend the refrigerator for comfort. But the minute he lays his hands on food, he hears a now familiar voice ordering him to put it down. It is Captain Marks, who is quickly joined by Commander Marks, and Big Bob Marks. When Bobby protests that they are all only figments of his imagination, Commander Marks astutely points out that that means Bobby is stuck with them. And so he is. He closes the refrigerator door, winner of that bout.

On Saturday Bobby's mother takes him shopping for clothes in the city. There they meet Mr. Marks at a department store and head for an area in the basement demeaningly called "Huskytown." Once there, the parents' normal roles are reversed: Mr. Marks becomes Bobby's defender, arguing that since the boy has lost weight, he should have some nice pants for a change as an incentive to stay slim. Mrs. Marks refuses to be convinced, however, pointing out that if Bobby gains weight, it is she who will have to alter the trousers. This leads to the usual argument, which rages, in one form or another, all the way back to the lake. This time, however, several important truths are revealed: When Mrs. Marks urges Bobby to have a rich piece of cake for dessert, Mr. Marks angrily tells her to leave the boy alone, that she has been pushing food into him for years. Since we know that she had also tried to persuade Bobby to have a dish of ice cream earlier that day as a reward—like the cake—we now realize that Mr. Marks is undoubtedly justified in his criticism. More importantly Bobby, reflecting on the fact that his father had championed buying him nice pants, realizes that for the first time the parent has demonstrated confidence in him. This inspires Bobby to refuse the cake and, he vows to himself, anything else that might lead him back to "Huskytown." This time the reader believes Bobby means it. And has won another bout.

Bobby and his parents arrive home just in time to interrupt a dramatic confrontation between Pete and his father, who has discovered that Pete is still seeing Michelle against his wishes. When Mr. Marino refers to Michelle as "that trampy daughter of yours," Mr. Marks furiously goes for the bigger man's throat. Michelle runs into the house sobbing, and Bobby, following her, demonstrates his newfound maturity by comforting his older sister for the first time. Bobby has just won another bout.

All of these triumphs dramatically set the stage for Bobby's final test. It begins ominously when Jim Smith approaches Bobby the following Friday to warn him that Willie has been drinking all week, working himself up to a violent confrontation. Bobby has the good sense to be apprehensive, and when he spots Willie's car on the way home that afternoon, he first hides and then hightails it to Marino's beach club, which he finds deserted except for Joanie, who is now working there, and Pete.

No sooner does Joanie agree to persuade Pete to give Bobby a ride home than Willie shows up brandishing a .22 rifle and wildly talking about taking Bobby back to the island to finish what he had started. Before this can happen, however, Jim Smith shows up, again not like a movie-clichéd U.S. Cavalry but, realistically, as someone who is aware of what has been transpiring and is concerned that his cousin not get himself in any more trouble than he is in already. At first Jim tries flattery to dissuade Willie from his threatened course of action, but Rumson is unmoved and launches another shrilly bigoted tirade, concluding by ominously aiming the rifle at Bobby's chest.

Time, obviously, for a more drastic measure than flattery.

Unfortunately the one Lipsyte chooses is right out of a gangster movie of the 1930s or 1940s. "Go ahead and kill 'im, Willie," Jim shouts, "go ahead, you brought enough grief to your Ma, might as well really fix her good this time, give her a stroke, too" (222). The blatantly clichéd, cinematic sentimentality of Jim's invoking Willie's mother is partially redeemed by a litany of Willie's failures, which he then brutally recites. From the passion with which Willie blames others for the miseries of his life, it is obvious that he is keenly aware of his own culpability and personal responsibility for his many failures. Hearing them recited now is probably like receiving a series of body blows. It also makes a kind of sense that this denouement should have been borrowed from a hundred B-movies, since Bobby's own sensibility has been largely formed by the movies—a fact revealed not only in his imagined alter ego, Captain Marks, a figure borrowed from a John Wayne movie, but in countless other references to films that Bobby has seen and that inspire courses of action to him (trying to kick Willie in the groin on the island being another example). But nevertheless this particular moment is robbed of some honest drama by its lack of invention and the invoking of a character whom the reader has never met and who, therefore, is not a person but only a label.

This criticism aside, what happens after that *is* fine and authentic, and serves as a viable catalyst for the book's memorable climax. Weakened by Smith's verbal attack, Willie gives his cousin the rifle and allows himself to be led away. Once his and Jim's backs are turned, Pete, who has been standing by in cowed silence, suddenly becomes brave. He runs after the two, leaps on their backs and sends them crashing to the dock. Smith rolls away, but Willie, caught off guard, is more vulnerable to Pete's attack. He is grabbed by the throat and lifted in the air. How badly he might have been injured by Pete is moot, since Smith breaks up the fight by pointing Willie's rifle at the two, and Pete (sensibly) backs off. Now unarmed and unmanned, Willie frantically does the only thing he can think to do to reassert *his* manhood. He puts his head down and charges at what he thinks is an easy target: Bobby.

The two fall to the dock, and Bobby does the only thing *he* can think to do: with Willie locked in his arms, he rolls off the dock and into the water, where he knows he will have the advantage. And, indeed, as he continues to hold Willie underwater and feels his antagonist's struggles weaken, he experiences an unaccustomed surge of triumph. Both the physical reality and the symbolic importance of Bobby's subterranean struggle and victory are appropriate and nicely handled, but any enjoyment of victory is short-lived.

For Jim now jumps into the water, separates the two boys, and pushes Willie onto the dock, where his defeat is so manifestly abject and pathetic that Bobby, watching Willie's skinny body shake and heave, suddenly feels sick himself. Pete feels no such qualms, however, and, commandeering the rifle, he once again attempts to take charge of the situation. But appropriately—now that we understand the lifeguard's essential weakness—he only succeeds in making himself look foolish. Smith simply stares at Pete in disgust and, loading the now helplessly retching Willie into his truck, drives away.

Not recognizing his own humiliation and exulting in his "triumph," Pete tries to launch a celebration and dubs Bobby a "hero" for having given Willie something he will never forget. But Bobby now sees his former hero with new eyes. "Why'd you have to do it, Pete?" he sadly asks. "'Do what?' He didn't know what I was talking about" (228). The scene ends as Bobby realizes that Pete will never understand the reality of what has transpired.

Bobby understands, however. He understands the emptiness of his previous notions of masculinity and the fatuousness of his movie-fueled fantasies of manhood. Being a man, he now perceives, is more than pretending to like baseball or posturing like Pete Marino. And it is certainly more than Willie Rumson–type bullying. Bobby may not yet fully know what being a man is, but he clearly knows what it is *not*: it is not taking advantage of those who are weaker or more vulnerable than you are.

Bobby's physical transformation—his weight loss and the hardening of his body through demanding physical labor—is a significant and gratifying accomplishment, for both Bobby and for the reader, who empathetically shares his sense of accomplishment, but its real significance is, once again, its symbolic value. For Bobby's true transformation is his newfound maturity, his self-confidence, his sense of self-worth, and his emergent strength of character. It is these that give him the courage in the last chapter to finally confront Dr. Kahn, to demand the fair wage that should have been his all along, and to recognize that he has earned this through his own efforts. "You didn't do it, Dr. Kahn. I did it," he tells his blustering employer (230).

Bobby's summer has been fat with challenges, and he has met them all, including the largest: he has obtained a demanding job on his own, and, despite all the obstacles, he has kept it. And that has made all the difference—a difference neatly epitomized in the last two sentences of the book: "I like summer. All the seasons are terrific" (232).

As a work of fiction, *One Fat Summer* is clearly superior to *Jock and Jill* and shares the same strengths as *The Contender*: believable, fully realized characters, thematic coherence, and the closely observed verisimilitude of a memorable setting. The boxing ring and New York's mean streets provided the milieu of *The Contender*, of course. But the rural resort community of *One Fat Summer*, though vastly different, is equally well realized. It is also nicely fixed in a historic moment—the early 1950s. Lipsyte himself calls this book and the two other Bobby Marks novels that would follow his "historical novels."

Reviewers were almost universally enthusiastic about the author's easy evocation of this era, and it is worth taking a moment to examine how Lipsyte established this chronological aspect of his setting. The most obvious element is his repeated mention of popular songs and singers of this pre–rock-and-roll era: "Little White Cloud That Cried" by Johnnie Ray, "Any Time" by Eddie Fisher (Bobby's favorite singer), "Tennessee Waltz," "Come On-a My House," "Mockin' Bird Hill," and "My Truly, Truly Fair." Sometimes, of course, Lipsyte makes these references perform double duty for him, as when Bobby demonstrates his iconoclastic wit by poking fun at the music. Hearing Michelle playing yet another Johnny Ray record about crying, he thinks she may drown in her room if she keeps playing those songs. Other cultural references abound: the names of movie stars like John Wayne and Humphrey Bogart are routinely invoked, of course, but also those of Broadway shows ("New Faces of 1952") and of radio and TV performers and programs (radio newscaster Gabriel Heatter and *I Love Lucy*, for example).

Topical references are also present: polio is mentioned, and Bobby reacts with the authentic fear that any young person of that era would have experienced; when Mrs. Marks asks if it were Joanie who has just telephoned, Bobby sarcastically replies, "No, it was Ike. He wanted to know if I like him" (145). ("I Like Ike" was, of course, the memorable 1951 campaign slogan of President Dwight D. ("Ike") Eisenhower.) Also represented is the unfortunately too-easy bigotry espoused by people like Willie Rumson and Pete Marino's father in this decade before the Civil Rights movement.

Though less easy to specify, the whole tone of the book is redolent of the fifties. The *New York Times* reviewer noted, "The time is 1952, and Lipsyte mingles the flavor of the era in his prose; the issues, tastes and expressions of the day echo through the narrative"[1] Another reviewer hailed the dialogue ("a lot of pseudo-cool 'ranking out'") and claimed that it "catches the early 1950's better than all the references to ponytails, polio and pop songs of the era."[2] Though the book's theme of self-transformation is timeless, in a sense it, too, epitomizes the fifties—perhaps the last historic moment when Americans were still naively optimistic about the possibility of positive progress and personal self-improvement (Norman Vincent Peale's *The Power of Positive Thinking* was published in 1952, the same year as Bobby's "fat summer").

In the most basic sense the success of the book in evoking the ethos of this more innocent era is due to the fact that it is Lipsyte's own story. He was there. He lived it. Like Bobby he, too, was a fat fourteen-year-old in 1952. His parents, like Bobby's, had a vacation home on a lake in upstate New York (in the town of Monroe, where they now live in retirement), and his father "couldn't wait to get out of the City on the weekends." It was also there that Lipsyte underwent a self-transformation nearly identical to Bobby's: "That summer, I left most of the worst of me on the lawn of a curmudgeon who paid me a dollar an hour to mow, trim, rake and clean the land around his country house. He delighted in humiliating me, especially in front of his guests, for blades of grass I failed to cut. I hated him then and I love him now. When I returned to school that September, my clothes hung on me like dead sails. I remember standing on the scale for what seemed like hours, smiling down at 168" ("Prisoner," 32).

Though Lipsyte claims that "Bobby is an idealized version of me—smarter, braver, better looking," the two clearly have much in common, though not perhaps their parents. For Lipsyte flatly states in this regard that "there's no relation between those parents and mine. I don't think my father ever noticed whether I was fat or not fat." On the other hand, when he goes on to mention that his father was "distanced emotionally," one cannot help but think of Bobby's father. And his recent description of his parents in his *American Health* column, "Close Encounters," could be lifted from the pages of *One Fat Summer* (except that the real-life parents are now elderly, of course). Consider: "My mother is eighty-three, physically active and mentally sharp. She speaks her mind. Her heart is on her sleeve. . . . My father is eighty-seven, physically active and mentally sharp. He keeps his own counsel . . . cool and veiled. . . . I can't always read him."[3]

As for other characters: Lipsyte, like Bobby, has a sister, but Lipsyte's is seven years younger than he (Michelle is four years older than Bobby). However, Michelle is studying psychology in college, and Lipsyte's sister grew up to be a psychiatrist (he claims that he routinely calls her whenever he has a disturbing dream). When asked if he had a real-life friend like Joanie, Lipsyte laughs and replies, "Apparently three, because three women have come forward claiming to be Joanie."

Perhaps because *One Fat Summer* was so clearly Lipsyte's most personal book to the time of its writing, it is understandable that, as he told one interviewer, "When I finished, I didn't feel a lot of relief. I was depressed, like I'd moved out of the neighborhood and left one of my friends behind" (Kenny, 286). As it turned out, Lipsyte's sovereign remedy for this "departure" depression was to figuratively revisit the neighborhood and rediscover his friend there by writing two more books about him: *Summer Rules* and *The Summerboy*, published by Harper and Row in 1981 and 1982, respectively.

In fact, Lipsyte had hoped to write yet a fourth Bobby Marks novel in which he would take Bobby into the army at the end of the fifties. "I was going to have something bad happen to him at college. . . . You know, in those days if something bad happened to you, you could jump into the Army. I was going to put him into a Reserve Group where they have six months of active duty, and then I would have ended it with his being a summer copy boy at the [New York] *Times*." Similarly Lipsyte hoped to write a sequel to *Jock and Jill* in which a movie is made of Hector's life, and Jack, "agonizing over whether to turn pro or not, is invited out to Hollywood to play a bit part."

Though nothing came of either of these ideas, Lipsyte finally got a character to Hollywood in his 1993 novel, *The Chief*, and, in the same book, he also brought Bobby Marks back as a now adult character, though not in the role of summer soldier but as a professor of writing, one of whose students, Martin Witherspoon, is the son of Bill Witherspoon, Alfred Brooks's mentor in *The Contender*. To compound the irony, careful readers of *One Fat Summer* will recognize Spoon as the boy who was a student of Bobby's mother when she was a volunteer teacher in Harlem and whom she once brought to the Marks's summer home for a disastrous vacation from the mean streets of Harlem.

No wonder that Lipsyte refers to his characters as his "repertory company." The curtain rises on them again in the next chapter.

7. Of Rules and the Boy

"A real man's job."

Lipsyte may already have been thinking of his characters as members of his "repertory company" as early as 1981, for many of the characters who appeared in *One Fat Summer* return for an encore appearance in its sequel, *Summer Rules*. Of the former's major characters only Pete Marino is absent, his parents having sold their beach club and moved away. (Joanie is in Europe when the book begins but will return to Rumson Lake later in the story.)

The year is 1954 and the now sixteen-year-old Bobby is, happily, still cocky, wisecracking, and slender despite his mother's unchanging determination to fill him up with food. His father, similarly, is still determined that Bobby will find work at a summer camp. "I hear there's an opening at Happy Valley," he announces at dinner and Bobby answers with—what else—a wisecrack: "'Better close it quick,' I cracked, 'before all that happiness spills out.'"[1]

As before, Bobby has other pressing plans that would preclude his working at a camp. This time around he intends to get "a real man's" job working on a landscape gardening crew with Jim Smith, who has become his friend through the discovery of their mutual love of cowboy movies, something they share with Lipsyte himself, who fondly recalls going to westerns as a boy with his father, an experience he calls "our baseball games." Bobby's choice of job will, he thinks, nourish his continuing plans to become a writer by feeding him "the kind of exciting adventures I needed to become a writer like Ernest Hemingway" (1). (The idea

77

of the writer as hero is one that fired Lipsyte's own adolescent imagination, though his role model was not Hemingway but the author-adventurer Richard Halliburton: "First you swim the roiling croc-infested waters, then you write about it."[2]

Beyond its suggestion of heroic aspirations, this thought also reveals that, for Bobby, a writer's inspiration is to be found in his life experiences, not in his imagination or intellect. Like his alter ego, Lipsyte has also observed that what may set him apart from other ("hothouse") writers for young adults is the enriching of his writing life by his experiences "out in the world" as a print and electronic journalist. (Hemingway was a working journalist at one time, of course, as was Lipsyte's own favorite young adult author, Robert Cormier.)

To give credit where it is due, Bobby does, on one occasion, appreciatively wonder where a writer would be without his imagination. But this testimonial is compromised by his subsequent action when, instead of using his imagination to solve the problem that has inspired the thought, he simply borrows the plot of Steinbeck's short story "The Red Pony." (As previously noted, Steinbeck was Lipsyte's favorite author when he was growing up.)

An increasingly dedicated would-be writer, at any rate, Bobby has started carrying a pencil and a notebook so that he can write down any good line that occurs to him. Since a good line, for Bobby, is one that is passionately overwritten, quoting these gives Lipsyte an opportunity to poke gentle fun at Bobby's exuberant adolescent style: "Every diamond sparkling on the water might just as well have been a cold pebble in my mouth now that Pedro was dead and the girl was in the clutches of the bandits" (9).

As before, Bobby also finds inspiration for his behavior and reactions in movie plots and in motion picture actors' personal style and conduct, especially those of Humphrey Bogart and Alan Ladd, whose most famous movie, *Shane*, is Bobby's favorite (a fact that will play a part in *The Summerboy*, too). In this same context of the interplay of real life and the imagined reality of fiction and motion pictures, Lipsyte revisits and expands one of the major themes of *One Fat Summer*: the casual presence of lies (or polite fictions) in family life, and the ways in which these compromise personal integrity. Indeed, the very title *Summer Rules* refers to the automatic relaxation of rules of conduct—including truth telling—during the lazy, laid-back days of summer.

Lipsyte introduces this theme early on, when it becomes obvious that Mr. Marks is finally going to have his way in the matter of Bobby's summer employment. But to get Bobby the job in question, Michelle, who is already employed at the camp, has to lie about his age (three years earlier she had lied about *her* age, too). Michelle's lie will introduce the usual tangled web of deceit, particularly as it regards Bobby's budding relationship with Sheila, a girl he meets at the camp, who naturally thinks he is old enough to drive (he is not) and to be going to college in the fall (he is not).

Furthermore, once Bobby is ensconced at the camp, part of the book's plot will revolve around the production of a play (art imitating and altering life). When Michelle publicly chastises Bobby for lying to one of the children in his charge (the child had climbed to the roof of the camp casino and obstinately refused to come down; to frighten him into compliance Bobby had pretended to see a buzzard that, he claimed, would peck the boy's eye out, as a similar bird had done to the red pony in John Steinbeck's story), the play's director—overhearing—responds, "Nonsense. Life is playacting and playacting is lying, ergo, life is lying" (51). Still later, Sheila and Bobby argue about the ethicality of lying to the same young boy. "Illusion, not lies," Bobby corrects, starting to add, "In this play by Pirandello . . ." but he is cut off by Sheila, who dismissively asserts, "This is real life, not plays" (99).

For sixteen-year-old Bobby "real life" revolves around two inevitably interrelated matters, both of which are symbolic of every teen's desire for adult independence: getting his first driver's license and having his first sexual experience. For Bobby, these are milestones on the continuing journey he began in *One Fat Summer* toward attaining the goal of real manhood. Indeed, at one critical point in his new relationship with Sheila, Bobby, despairingly aware that he must still rely on his older sister to drive him everywhere, wonders, "When was I going to be in the driver's seat? Of my own life?" (119). This could be Lipsyte speaking of his own adolescent life. He recalled in a recent interview that he had felt isolated as an overweight "summer boy." "But then after I lost my weight and got my driver's license, it was catch-up time. I think there was a period of some years when I didn't read a book. I didn't do anything but chase, run around, just have a great time."

Mr. Marks, who is giving Bobby driving lessons, no doubt understands that this is Bobby's unstated ambition, too, and he characteristically admonishes, "Control, Robert, control is the secret word." "Control," Bobby thinks. "Sometimes when he said it, I wasn't sure if he was talking only about driving, or Life, too" (35).

So long as Bobby's new friend Sheila is in the driver's seat of their emerging relationship, there is no doubt that Bobby's "ambition" to score sexually will be controlled here, too. Wisecracking, brittle, tough-minded, Sheila is more than a match for Bobby. She is also the only one who, seemingly, can control her cousin, young Harley Bell, the emotionally disturbed son of the camp's owner. Since Bobby is the newest counselor, Harley has been assigned to his group. The only good thing about this for Bobby is that his custody of Harley brings him and Sheila together. In fact, their commonality of interest leads to a developing relationship and Bobby's first kiss, which he describes with his characteristic understatement: "When we broke for air, thunder roared in my ears and fires raged over my body" (84).

Like her brother, Michelle is also infatuated. The object of her affection is a fellow camp counselor and college student named Jerry Silver, one of Lipsyte's less sterling characterizations. Though the text leaves some small margin for ambiguity, there is very little doubt that Jerry is a homosexual (and in conversation Lipsyte confirms that he is). As such, he is unfortunately less a character than a collection of gay stereotypes, which begin with his job: this self-dramatizing twenty-one-year-old is the camp's music and dramatics counselor, of course. "Jerry seemed to know the words of every song ever written, especially Broadway show tunes," Bobby observes (80). For Jerry, who refers to himself as "Silverstar," all the world is a stage, and he is always at its center whether he is self-consciously tossing his "lion's mane of brown hair" or bringing a melodramatic flair to the normally prosaic act of smoking a cigarette.

When he talks, Jerry seems to be giving dramatic readings of simple, declarative sentences: "Mi-chelle. You look fab-u-lous." Or—more annoyingly—he employs cutely coy locutions: Bobby is never Bobby or Bob, he is "Brother Roberto." Sheila is "Our Lady of the Lunches." "Martinis" are "martoonis." When congratulated for an act of heroism, " ''Tis nothing,' said Jerry. He tossed his lion's mane hair" (137).

For Bobby, Jerry is little more than his sister's annoying boyfriend until, one evening at a party, the older boy makes a pass at him, squeezing his leg and offering him a private audition for a part in the camp's summer musical. Bobby is terrified, jumping up and running away from Jerry and into the house, where he pours himself a large martooni for courage and then, hearing a voice that he thinks might be Jerry's, plunges into the nearby woods.

Though Bobby may wonder the next day, through the agonizing haze of his first, rite-of-passage hangover, if Jerry had really made a pass at him, there will be little doubt in the reader's mind, since Lipsyte has stacked the deck against Jerry. In an earlier chapter, for example, when Jerry coyly promises to make Michelle a star or, failing that, to just make her, the musclebound athletic director sneeringly says, "That'll be the day" (17).

For an author who is usually the model of intelligent and empathetic enlightenment, such a cruelly clichéd characterization is surprising and is hardly redeemed by Lipsyte's later arguable establishment of Jerry as a hero when a fire threatens the lives of his theatrical company. One says "hardly," since this act of heroism is not witnessed by the reader. Rather, it is reported, gushingly, by Michelle, who is enamored of Jerry and is, therefore, hardly a reliable witness. Moreover the act visits no discernable change on Jerry's character nor on Bobby's attitude toward him.

The unfortunate fact remains that Jerry, as the only gay character in the book, offers readers the same negative stereotypes of gays that a Willie Rumson might espouse (in *One Fat Summer* he derogatorily calls Bobby "faggot" whenever he is particularly angry). And earlier in this book Jim Smith, another Rummie, has warned Bobby to be careful that the Happy Valley counselors do not turn him into a "queer." These are unfortunate attitudes, but in Lipsyte's defense, they are not his own but rather his characters'. As such, they are perfectly consistent with the unfortunate attitudes toward homosexuality that prevailed in the 1950s when the story takes place. More significantly, they belong in a book that has as its theme sexual awakening and the adolescent's uncertain struggle to establish sexual identity.

At the outset, Bobby's attitudes about sex are the product not only of the time and the society in which he lives but also of his observation of those, like Jim Smith, whom he rightly or wrongly admires. Since Bobby is a reader and would-be writer, they may also be a product of the macho posturings of his favorite author and writing role model, Ernest Hemingway. (When he first meets Sheila's Aunt Rose, he introduces himself as "Robert Jordan," the protagonist of Hemingway's *For Whom the Bell Tolls*.)

Ultimately Bobby's ideas about sex are inextricably part of his evolving ideas about what it means to be a man. Like every adolescent boy, his life is a daily struggle to define the meaning of manhood. In *One Fat Summer* he has already rejected the mindless model of Pete Marino. He finds similarly distasteful Al Rapp, the camp's athletic director, who hides his insecurities behind a facade of muscular flesh that he takes elaborate care *not* to hide. Like Pete Marino, Al always wears as few clothes as possible, and whenever he talks, he self-consciously flexes his muscles.

By now Bobby is both mature and experienced enough to see through this posturing facade and to underscore his insight with his characteristic wit: noting that Al flexes his muscles when he talks as if the act were punctuation, he wonders if the other boy had determined with a mirror "which muscles were commas and which were periods" (14). On the other hand, he continues to admire Jim Smith, though not necessarily for the right reasons. Smith has promised to teach him the art of souping up a car and to introduce him to the honky-tonk world of country bars.

Though the point is never explicitly made, Bobby may also find Jim attractive because his laconic style is reminiscent of the strong and silent screen presences of Bobby's favorite actors, Bogart and Ladd. As to the question of why Jim would tolerate Bobby's adolescent friendship (aside from their mutual appreciation of western movies), Bobby unwittingly supplies the answer by explaining that he has promised to introduce Smith to the summer girls whom the older boy could otherwise only admire from a distance. For Jim women are little more than objects for sexual gratification. And since Bobby has accurately described him and the other members of the landscaping crew as "rough guys who drag raced and hunted and had girl friends who went all the way" (1), it is not surprising that Jim speaks of women with contempt.

Bobby's own initial attraction to Sheila—she of the "dazzlingly" green eyes and black curls—is purely physical: "The heat I had felt on my back spilled into my stomach, my groin, my legs" (31). Bobby's first sexual stirrings have already been reported in *One Fat Summer* in the form of a sexual fantasy (the Invisible Boy going into the girl's locker room), an instance of masturbation, and a wet dream about Joanie. But this is Bobby's first instance of prompt arousal on meeting a girl.

Significantly the chapter in which this happens is immediately followed by a contrapuntal chapter in which Bobby receives his first driving lesson from his father, who sternly tells him that driving is a matter of learning control. Even without Mr. Marks's observation most readers will have already understood the metaphorical value of Bobby's learning to drive, of beginning to steer his own life in the direction it will go, of controlling his own destiny. His sexual maturation and his attendant understanding of how sexuality fits into the puzzle of manhood will be an important part of this rite of passage. For the moment, however, Bobby is blissfully unaware of these serious considerations, enjoying, instead, the visceral pleasure of the physical act of driving and of imagining a beautiful girl in the passenger seat.

Bobby is determined that that girl will be Sheila.

There is, of course, more to manhood than sexual maturity, and Lipsyte ingeniously marries Bobby and Sheila's burgeoning relationship with Bobby's driving lessons and the opportunity they offer for serious conversation with his father. These reintroduce the book's second primary theme: truth telling as an exercise in personal integrity and maturity.

At the same party at which Jerry has made a pass, Bobby has gotten drunk for the first time. This is more than the obligatory rite-of-passage; it leads to Bobby's being grounded and his driving lessons being canceled—not because he has come home drunk but because his father thinks he has been lied to. When this misunderstanding has been cleared up, Mr. Marks reminds Bobby, "You're back in the driver's seat today because you didn't lie to me . . . lying is never justified. Don't you agree?" (85). When Bobby does not, Mr. Marks counters: "Some people think that when they're in a foreign country or dealing with women or on vacation that the usual standards don't apply." "Like summer rules," Bobby says. "No such thing," Mr. Marks replies. "There are no special situations when it comes to the truth" (87).

Of course, Bobby's earlier creation of just such a "special situation" by lying to young Harley Bell has already jeopardized his relationship with Sheila once. Shortly another lie, the one about his age, will bring a second crisis to their relationship. Although he is "almost positive" that he has not actually told Sheila that he is going to college in the fall (he is not, of course), she has somehow formed the assumption that he is. Bobby never even considers telling her the truth, since to do so would mean revealing his true age, and he is convinced that if Sheila found that out, she would leave him. Inevitably Bobby finds himself resorting to a duplicitous strategy of telling half-truths or lying with his silence. Neither of these satisfies Sheila, and the two teenagers have their first argument.

Later that evening Bobby tries to comfort himself by thinking that Sheila is a nice girl who only wants assurance that he cares for her as a person and is interested in a long-term relationship. "Of course," he concludes cynically, "that didn't mean I had to tell her the truth. Whatever that was" (105). The truth is that Bobby does *not* care for Sheila as a person, though the reader may realize this before he does. During their earlier argument

Sheila has confirmed that she has let Bobby take unprecedented physical liberties. "Big deal," Bobby callously thinks, "after two weeks she finally let me reach inside her blouse to rub her brassiere" (102).

On their next date Sheila rebuffs Bobby's advances, demanding to know if she means nothing to him but an opportunity for physical intimacy. Shamed into spending time on conversation instead of kissing, Bobby is appalled at what he perceives to be Sheila's ignorance. Dismayed, he wonders how he could spend the summer with a girl "who barely knows who Hemingway is" (113). Sheila, blissfully unaware of the sea change in Bobby's attitude, puts her arms around his neck. "See?" she says with unconscious irony, "We can have an intelligent discussion" (114).

While Bobby's relationship with Sheila is changing, circumstances at the camp are changing, too. Bobby, at his mother's suggestion, has gotten Harley involved with special activities—a position on the camp baseball team plus a role in Jerry's play. This works well at first—Harley is now too busy to be a burden on Bobby—but soon it becomes obvious that the already emotionally fragile young boy is now so physically and emotionally overextended by these taxing activities that he may be heading for a nervous breakdown. What to do about it?

Sheila, possessively calling Bobby "my psychiatrist," tells him he will think of something. Far from being reassured, Bobby reports that he feels even more trapped than before. Meanwhile Bobby's old bête noire, Willie Rumson, has shown up, newly released from prison, where he has been serving time for setting fire to Dr. Kahn's toolshed. While incarcerated, he has received electric shock treatments and some kind of mysterious injections. As a result, he is no longer a threatening presence but, instead, a pathetic combination of zombie and walking zucchini. Improbably Jim brings Willie with him when he comes to the camp to do a landscaping job. Even more improbably Willie is left to wander about the camp at will drinking beer and idly flicking his cigarette lighter off and on. Willie's playing with fire will remind most readers of Harley's earlier established passion for playing with matches. In a heavy-handed scene, Al Rapp, the musclebound athletic coordinator, physically assaults the now helpless Willie—as Pete did in *One Fat Summer*. When Bobby challenges this, Rapp calls Willie a firebug and portentously adds, "You want him to do the same thing to that firetrap of a casino he did to Dr. Kahn's house?" (120).

It becomes obvious to the reader that the stage is being set for something more ominous than the camp production of *The King and I* when, a paragraph later, Bobby drags Harley out of that same casino where he is rehearsing and tries to persuade the boy to choose between the ball team and the play. To continue doing both, Bobby reasons, is "too much for one person." Harley refuses to choose, however, and, with wistful portentousness, sighs, "I wish one of them would disappear . . . then I wouldn't have to choose" (122). Having been lied to once by Bobby, Harley refuses to believe his reassurances and runs away, leaving Bobby behind, hoisted on the petard of his own penchant for prevarication. Sheila finds him there (in the next paragraph) and challenges him, in turn, to make a choice of his own by telling her the truth about his feelings for her. Bobby, like Harley, is unable to do this, and the chapter ends with his waffling and walking into the casino to escape further dealings with her.

By now it is clear to both the reader and Bobby that his relationship with Sheila is a sad mistake. For some reason, however, Lipsyte belabors the obvious by then bringing Joanie home from Europe for a one-chapter, cameo appearance, just long enough for her to tell Bobby that she has fallen in love with a college student named Stewart whom she met in Paris. Bobby realizes that he is jealous of their relationship, which is based on intellectual equality and mutual understanding, unlike his with Sheila. Extraneous or not, this chapter does further set the stage for the dramatic climax to follow.

It begins with Bobby's being invited by Sheila to a picnic. Having plied Bobby with food, she declares she now loves him and does not want to lose him and to prove it, announces that she wants to go to "make-out island" with him, the same place where Bobby had been dumped, naked, by the hapless Willie Rumson in *One Fat Summer*. Bobby agrees but is disturbed to find the passage there as frighten-

ing and life-changing as it had been the first time. Considering his
fear, Bobby realizes, powerfully, that he is not yet ready to con-
summate his relationship with Sheila. With that understanding, he
also realizes that Sheila is equally scared and reluctant but mis-
guidedly thinks that agreeing to have sex with him is the only way
she can save their relationship. For Bobby, however, having sex
would be an act of commitment to this girl for whom he no longer
cares. But he is afraid to tell her this. Rather than confront this
fear, he instead angrily wonders what is wrong with him, recalling Jerry's advance and thinking that perhaps the older boy
sensed that he is "some kind of queer" (135).

In an earlier chapter Michelle had loftily explained to Bobby
that she and Jerry have a platonic relationship, implying that is
more mature and satisfying than the purely physical one Bobby
is enjoying with Sheila. Bobby, stung, hotly retorted, "At least we
do what real men and women do" (104). By now, however, it is
obvious that Bobby is having serious second thoughts about the
validity of his earlier beliefs and the limited part the sexual act
plays in defining what "real men and women" are.

At the last moment, just as they set foot on the island, the two
are saved from themselves—or each other—when they spot a raging fire on the mainland, up the Happy Valley hill. They immediately return to camp to discover that, sure enough, the casino has
burned to the ground. It takes no great powers of deduction for
Bobby to realize that Harley, unable to choose between the baseball team and the play, has, instead, chosen to make one of them
"go away" by setting fire to the casino. Despite his misgivings, he
is persuaded by Harley's uncle, the camp director, not to tell anyone what he knows. At this critical moment Bobby sees Willie
being taken away in handcuffs by the police, who presume it is he
who has set the fire. Since Bobby and Sheila have earlier stum-
bled across Willie dead drunk and passed out at the dock, Bobby
knows that Willie is innocent. But he is, once again, persuaded
not to tell the police. When he does later tell his story to Michelle
and still later to his mother, both agree that he should remain
silent. Improbable as this may seem, it is important for dramatic
purposes that they should promote a conspiracy of silence, since

it sets the stage for Bobby's last driving lesson with his father the next day and a final discussion that will force Bobby to make his own choice.

Bobby initiates the dialogue by asking if remaining silent when you have knowledge of an offense could ever be construed as a lie. Mr. Marks is impatient with such sophistry, insisting there are no summer rules regarding the truth. Bobby persists: "But if you don't tell it, it's not a lie, right?" (147). By now slightly exasperated, Mr. Marks flatly declares that either one lies or one tells the truth and claiming you are doing one, when in reality you are doing the other, is only lying to yourself. This is what Bobby needs to hear, and it serves as the catalyst for his decision to drive into town and tell the police his story.

With this most important issue settled, the book's other narrative problems are quickly resolved. Willie is released from jail and sent upstate to stay with one of his brothers. Harley and Sheila are whisked away by Harley's father. Bobby is fired from the camp, and Michelle, to his surprise, quits in protest. And Bobby gets an unexpected ten-dollar tip from the mother of one of his campers. "I planned to spend the ten dollars on pencils, pads, and gasoline," Bobby reports, ending his story on a prophetic note (150).

The reviews of *Summer Rules* were nearly unanimous in their enthusiastic praise (one reviewer called it "altogether splendid"), but it seems clear, twelve years after its publication, that it is a less successful book than *One Fat Summer*. Its chief failing is the sense of contrivance that compromises its dramatic climax—the unnecessary chapter with Joanie, the heavy-handed scenes with Willie flicking his Zippo, Bobby and Sheila's too fortuitous stumbling over the passed-out ex-Marine, Bobby's mother's casually encouraging him to lie, and so forth. Even more compromising is the unbelievable transformation of hard-headed Sheila into a dewy-eyed, would-be doxy, and the author's whisking her away after the fire to spare Bobby the pain of having to confront her and tell her the truth. Without this essential rite-of-passage the reader feels cheated. Also unresolved is the fact that Bobby has once again been taken advantage of by an employer. Near the beginning of the book Moe Bell, the camp director, manages to cheat Bobby out of the full counselor's wage and though Bobby, nearly in tears, acknowledges to the reader that he hates it when someone takes advantage of him, he never does anything about it. In fact, when he is fired at book's end, he does not even collect his reduced salary, since Moe claims Bobby is in breach of contract for having lied about his age. The reader does not know what to make of this, since the point is never pursued.

Nevertheless, the book does succeed handsomely as another humorous evocation of the fifties. The relationship between Bobby and his father is nicely handled, and the metaphorical value of Bobby's driving lessons is seamlessly integrated into the narrative. Though secondary to the book's chief themes—the primary importance of truth telling in the passage to manhood and the secondary importance of sex in a meaningful relationship—Bobby's role as counselor to the campers in his charge is also nicely and believably handled. Bobby has continued to grow as a character and continues to appeal as a narrator. Most readers would agree with the reviewer who wrote, "I hope we have not heard the last of formerly fat Bobby."[3]

The Summerboy

In fact, Bobby apparently did use his ten-dollar tip to buy more paper and pencils, since, a year after the publication of *Summer Rules*, a third Bobby Marks novel, *The Summerboy*, was published (1982). In the interior chronology of the series two more years have passed; it is now the summer of 1956 and Bobby, eighteen, has just finished his freshman year in college. Sister Michelle is traveling in Europe; his father is preparing for a double-hernia operation, and Mom, who finally became a teacher in *Summer Rules*, is getting ready for the final month of her teaching year. Thus, with his sister absent and his parents distracted by their own concerns, there is no one to subject Bobby to the usual interrogation when he announces that he has taken a new summer job driving a truck for the Lenape Laundry.

The job is the fulfillment of a long-standing dream. As early as *One Fat Summer* Bobby had fantasized about becoming a truck driver, wondering, at fourteen, if he could ever be as cool as he imagines them to be. Four years later he still thinks they are cool and—at least in his fevered, eighteen-year-old fantasies—irresistible to attractive women.

Despite the painful lessons of his disastrous relationship with Sheila in *Summer Rules*, Bobby still is driven by dreams of sexual scoring. And his imagination is still fired by the actions of movie star heroes like Ladd and Bogart—though, in true college freshman fashion, he now thinks of them not as heroes but as antiheroes. Warned when he applies for a job as a truck driver for the Lenape Laundry that the rugged foreman, Bump Ennis, believes, like Willie Rumson, that summer residents are worthless, Bob stubbornly realizes that this is another reason to take the job; not only will it enable him to score with girls, it will give him a chance to show the year-round residents what a summerboy can do. "Then," he concludes wistfully, "I'd ride off, like Shane."[4] This character from the classic George Stevens western movie is Bobby's shining model of masculinity and stoic heroism. His continuing idealization of this character suggests, too, his lingering tendency to look for his identity in his body and his attendant desire to emulate a man "whose skin is a perfect fit and whose muscles obey every command."[5]

These romantic notions will be dramatically tested, however, for if the dialectical relationship of lies and truth has been a theme of Bobby's earlier adventures, so the arduous evolution of his understanding of the differences between adolescent, movie-inspired fantasies of heroism and the more pedestrian and painful heroics of real life will be the major theme of *The Summerboy*.

There are some areas of commonality, however, between "reel" and "real" life. The celluloid hero, as epitomized by Shane, is distinguished by his essential solitude. He must be an outsider so that, in his splendid, enforced isolation, he has only himself and his own resources to fall back on when challenged. Bobby, too, will need to test his own capacities and resources. As a summerboy he is already a de facto outsider. The necessary solitude is supplied by his sister's continuing absence and his father's surgery, which will confine both of his parents to the city. Accordingly this will be Bobby's first summer alone—and on his own.

His outsider status and the profound influence of motion pictures on his thinking are vividly dramatized at the outset when he reports for his first day of work and encounters the truck foreman, the redoubtable Bump Ennis for the first time. Ennis snarls, "When Bump says 'Jump!' you'll ask, 'How high?'" "It was right out of a corny war movie. I knew just how to answer. I shouted, 'I read you loud and clear, Bump'" (8).

But real life is not a movie, as Bobby will painfully learn, and here is his first lesson. Ennis caustically dismisses him as a wise guy and sends him to cool his heels in a corner. Bobby, though he immediately realizes his mistake, is incurably romantic. Watching the other drivers race for their trucks, he cannot resist thinking of war movies in which pilots scramble for their planes before the enemy attacks. He is not too busy fantasizing, though, to notice the women arriving for work: "uncomplicated country girls who enjoy simple, rustic fun, such as rolling in the hay" (9).

Bobby's patronizing objectification of women demonstrates vividly how much he still has to learn about the equality of the sexes. (He has earlier been pleased to notice that the women employees—unlike the men—do not have the trademark Indian head logo on the back of their uniforms. In his mind this makes the men special.) That he is not alone in his ignorance and his attitude—one of the other supervisors snorts that women do not understand men's problems—vividly underscores the sexism of the fifties setting. Not surprisingly Bobby will also discover that the women employees are paid substantially less than the men.

Happily Bobby's education in equality gets under way quickly. First he meets a firebrand named Diana. His initially chauvinistic, knee-jerk reaction—"Diana, goddess of the hunt. You can hunt me anytime, baby"—is quickly replaced by admiration for her independence and tough-mindedness (16). Secondly, after he has an accident the first time he tries to drive a truck, he is fired by the foreman. To his surprise, the tweedy laundry owner, Roger Sinclair, phones him at home and offers to rehire him on the condition that he spy on the other workers. When Bobby demurs, Sinclair cagily appeals to his manhood: "Where's the heroic spirit? Did you leave it at the movies?" (26).

Bobby rises to this bait and reluctantly agrees to return to the laundry only to find he has been banished to the sheet-folding detail, where he is partnered with a grandmotherly septuagenarian named "Lolly." Bobby's description of this new milieu is clever and demonstrates his evolving skill as a writer: watching two of the elderly women at work he notes, "They performed a little folding dance. . . . I thought of Margaret Mead. . . . The Sheet-Folding Dancers of Lenape. Maybe I'll write it up for *National Geographic*" (29).

Bobby is at first superior to his elderly partner, but he quickly changes his attitude as he discovers how physically taxing the work is. Soon enough it is Lolly who is complaining that it is Bobby who is slowing her down. His amusingly hyperbolic description of the increasingly painful rite-of-sheet-folding-passage is reminiscent of his early days mowing Dr. Kahn's monster lawn: "Wet heat turned my suede desert boots into blotting paper, rotting my toenails" (33). Lolly dryly interrupts his reverie to observe that he looks "a little flushed," and Bobby is still strong enough to reply with a wisecrack.

This kind of panache—some might call it bravado—helps Bobby survive the day, to stagger off home and fall into bed but not before three more important things have happened. First he witnesses an argument between the fiery Diana and Lolly's supervisor, Axel, about a dangerously leaking steam valve over Lolly's head. Second, in a related incident he discovers that the truck he was driving at the time of his earlier accident had faulty brakes and that this is symptomatic of the sorry state of repair that characterizes all of the equipment. Why? A driver named Ace cynically explains that everything is wrong with everything in the plant because Sinclair (the laundry's owner) simply does not care to have it repaired. Indeed, the callous Sinclair has already demonstrated his contempt for his employees by describing them to Bobby as "this dismal swamp of demented greasers, cockeyed wenches, and hayseed bar brawlers" (5).

Third, Bobby discovers that Diana suspects his (reluctant) complicity with Sinclair and that his fellow workers have started a pool, betting on how soon he will quit. Discouraged and disheartened, Bobby resolves to work out the week and then to resign. Relieved at having made his decision, he actually begins to enjoy the work and starts making mental notes for a novel. Recalling that writer Evan Hunter had once spent a week as a substitute teacher getting background material for his novel *The Blackboard Jungle*, Bobby facetiously decides he will call *his* "best-seller" *The Soapflake Inferno*.

By his scrupulous recording of the details of his work environment, Bobby demonstrates that he is still serious about becoming a writer and, moreover, understands the importance of careful observation and verisimilitude (a strength of Lipsyte's own writing, as we have already discussed). Nevertheless at week's end Bobby leaves the plant determined not to return, until his old friend Jim Smith, now working as a driver for the laundry, follows him and, unaware of Bobby's decision, tries to persuade him to quit (just as he and Willie had tried to persuade Bobby to quit his lawn mowing job in *One Fat Summer*). Bobby shrewdly realizes that Jim has been sent by Bump and stubbornly decides that he will keep his job after all.

A weekend and a party at Joanie's separate Bobby from his next work day, however. Bobby and Joanie have long since patched up the differences that separated them in the wake of their respective transformations in *One Fat Summer* and are, once again, the best of friends. In fact, their relationship is one of the nicest elements of the Bobby Marks novels in its demonstration to young readers that males and females can be equal partners in a friendship that is as rewarding as, though quite different from, a traditional "love" relationship. Bobby realizes that he can relax with Joanie, since they are platonic friends, and therefore he does not have to play "Captain Cool" with her.

Bobby is surprised to see Roger Sinclair arrive at Joanie's party and is even more surprised to see that the slender, Ivy

League–looking man has "such a dumpy wife" (57). Moreover her walk is unsteady (has she been drinking?), and her eyes are swollen and red as if she has been crying. (Is her marriage in trouble?) It is more likely the laundry business that is in trouble, since Joanie's father, a wheeler-dealer who is always looking for insider information, has taken Bobby aside earlier in the evening to ask him if Sinclair has been doctoring his financial accounts. Before Bobby knows it, Mr. Miller has pressed him into service as a spy in the corporate works.

Bobby laughs at being asked to spy on the person for whom he is already spying, but for the moment he is too busy being "Captain Cool" to pay much attention to these ironies. He is more interested in impressing Mignon and Marie, two beautiful young French exchange students. Thinking they are watching him and hoping to impress them with an acrobatic dive, Bobby springs off the dock, remembering too late that Mr. Miller has laid gravel over the mud bottom of the lake. The reader winces as Bobby's face slams into the gravel. Humiliated and hurting, he slips away from the party, but not before he notices Joanie and a man he cannot see in the darkness "talking and laughing in that jittery way people use when they've just met and they're enormously attracted to each other, but a little scared" (61).

Bobby makes it home, but after a painfully sleepless night he heads for the neighboring Bushkins' cottage for help. Dr. and Mrs. Bushkin are weekend fixtures of the community whom Bobby has known since he was small. And though it is still early in the morning, they receive Bobby with concerned cordiality and carefully tend his facial wounds. In the interior monologue that introduces the Bushkins, Bobby recalls his father's saying that the Bushkins' ordeal in World War II—they are among those Jews who escaped from Nazi Germany at the last possible moment—"still didn't excuse what Dr. Bushkin was doing now" (64).

This is a nice bit of foreshadowing, since the Bushkins will be involved later when Bobby's story takes an even more dramatic and dangerous turn. The mechanism for introducing them into the story—Bobby's accident—is also nicely plausible, as is the necessary re-establishment of Bobby and Joanie's friendship and the introduction of Joanie's secret suitor (though his identity will become obvious to the reader long before it does to Bob).

Unfortunately Lipsyte leaves plausibility at the door of the next chapter: it is now Monday, and Bobby, looking like forty miles of bad gravel road, reports to work. One glimpse of his face and Bump and the drivers presume—wrongly, of course—that Bobby has been in a fight at the Dew Drop Inn. Anxious to impress them, Bobby does nothing to correct their misapprehension, and inevitably, as it did with Sheila in *Summer Rules*, the situation gets out of hand. Before long the entire loading-dock crew is convinced that Bobby is a master of martial arts, and the increasingly unnerved Bobby finds himself challenged to a fight by a Neanderthal type named Cliff. At the last possible instant a baby-blue Cadillac roars dramatically into the yard.

It is Joanie. Her serendipitous arrival allows Bobby to demonstrate that he has not seen all those movies for nothing. Making a great show of magnanimously letting his antagonist off the hook ("I won't hurt you brother," he says, pumping the bewildered Cliff's paw), and seizing the moment, he vaults into the front seat of the Caddie and tells Joanie to "burn rubber outa here" (76).

As Lipsyte has already demonstrated in *Jock and Jill*, which was published the same year as *The Summerboy*, he is not above violating the integrity of the tone and form of his books for the sake of a melodramatic scene or three. This scene, while it is amusing, readable, and certainly not without suspense, is completely inconsistent with the realistic nature of what has preceded it. It strains even the most noncritical readers' credulity to ask them to believe that all, or even several, of these cynical, street-smart drivers would believe that Bobby had bested four toughs in a barroom brawl or that this intellectual, college-student summerboy is actually a master of martial arts.

And what is Joanie doing, appearing out of nowhere? Of course, the fact that Bobby notices one of the office windows open as soon as Joanie arrives and Roger Sinclair poke his face out to stare at the Caddie must surely reveal to everybody but Bob that Sinclair is Joanie's secret swain. In the very next chapter, though, Joanie is coyly protesting that she cannot tell Bob who "he" is. So why has she come to the laundry in the first place, and if her heart forced her to, why did she make such a public and dramatic entrance? And why, when she takes Bob back to the laundry does she insist on driving back into the yard and then "rubberneck as if she was trying to look through the windows?" (81).

Bobby does not know what to make of this, but Lipsyte does and resorts to a device he has employed before and will employ again: he attempts to defuse criticism of a plot weakness by calling attention to it. This time he disingenuously has Bobby think, "Who cares why she showed up in the nick of time? Be glad she did. An English instructor would scrawl DEUS EX MACHINA! for an unexplained, illogical rescue" (78–79). Ironically, anyone who has read Lipsyte's 1993 novel *The Chief*, in which a now adult Bob Marks appears as a visiting professor of writing, will know that the tough-minded Professor Marks would be the first one to scrawl such a criticism.

At any rate, the combination of Bob's bravado and Joanie's dramatic appearance have impressed Bump, and to his delight, Bobby finds himself out of the sheet-folding business and back behind the wheel of a truck. Actually he is only a swing helper, loading trucks and going along when a driver needs a hand, but he is overjoyed to finally be working with the men outside (which is to say, in the pecking order of the Lenape Laundry, inside).

Unfortunately this is one case where the exciting world of the imagination far outstrips the daily dreariness of real life. For Bobby quickly finds he has little in common with the other drivers, whose conversation consists of recycled sports talk, the daily boasting about how much they drank the night before, and "raunchy comments" about the women working inside the laundry. Such talk betrays how empty their lives are and how devoid their jobs are, too, of the romance with which Bob had invested them.

Only one prospect continues to excite him: the possibility of a relationship with Diana. However, she remains openly contemptuous of him not only as a tool of Sinclair but as a summer boy, an outsider, one of those transient people who passes through other people's lives, using them for personal gratification and then throwing them away "like Kleenex." Just as Sinclair has thrown away her father, who, Bobby learns, has been let go from his job as a driver after an accident left him paralyzed—an accident that could have been avoided if Sinclair had let Bump replace the bald tires on the truck.

Given this motivation, it is understandable that Diana continues to be passionate about correcting the dangerous working conditions at the laundry. Unfortunately she is the only one who is willing to translate passion into action. The men may complain about conditions, Bump may promise Diana he will do something, but it is obvious that nothing will happen, though Bobby, in an attempt to please Diana, at least tries twice to talk with Sinclair about the conditions. The first time, Sinclair breezily dismisses the topic. The second time the older man is openly contemptuous: "Are you playing *Shane*," he sneers, "riding in to save the sodbusters?" (122). Bobby does, of course, identify with Shane, but being confronted with this fantasy reinforces its distance from his real-life powerlessness, and he bitterly thinks of himself as being nothing but a tool of Sinclair.

For Bob the transformation from tool to authentic hero will require an act of significant, real-life courage. Joanie provides the opportunity when Bobby, exhausted by his second confrontation with Sinclair, drags himself home to find her waiting for him on the front steps. She confesses to him that she is pregnant and desperately asks for his help in arranging an abortion.

Bobby at first nervously suggests other options, but when it becomes clear that Joanie is determined to abort the fetus, Bobby settles down and says, simply, "We'll take care of it" (128). It is Bobby who then thinks of calling Dr. Bushkin, who, as the reader has suspected, is an abortionist, and it is Bobby who bravely drives Joanie into the city for the procedure, even though he realizes that this act makes him an accomplice to a crime—abortion having been, of course, an illegal act in the 1950s.

Bobby's heroism is made credible by the fact that, unlike the mindless bravado of the movie hero, it is compounded of equal parts of courage and, because it is rooted in an intellectual apprehension of the possible consequences of his act, fear. And it is realistically and honorably motivated by loyalty to and concern for his friend. When Bobby delivers Joanie to the door of Dr. Bushkin's office, she pleads with him to leave if anything goes wrong, so that he will not have a "blot" on his record. "Relax, kid," Bobby bravely reassures his friend, though he has trouble keeping his voice steady. "Blots look good on a writer's record" (133).

The three hours he must wait for Joanie's procedure to be completed are, for Bobby, an opportunity for serious introspection and for epiphany. The urgent reality of his present circumstance makes him realize, perhaps for the first time, the shallowness of Hollywood heroics—some make-believe guy [having] fake adventures" (134)—and he realizes, in this context, how many of his ideas have derived from the movies. Lipsyte dramatizes this realization beautifully by introducing an element of suspense-building misdirection worthy of an Alfred Hitchcock film. Since first arriving in the neighborhood of Dr. Bushkin's office, Bobby has been noticing a group of large women who apparently know each other. He thinks, at first, that they are watching him but puts it down to a guilty conscience until, later, he sees two of them near Dr. Bushkin's office and thinks, in panic, that there is going to be a raid. When the women finally approach him and give him a piece of paper, Bobby automatically thinks he is being handed an arrest warrant until he looks at the paper and discovers that it is, in reality, a flier advertising a church service. The women are not police but street missionaries.

Bobby's education in reality continues as, thinking of Joanie's lonely ordeal in Dr. Bushkin's office, he sees clearly how contemptible Roger Sinclair is in his habit of "taking advantage of every woman in his life," not just Joanie but also the women in the laundry. Bobby thinks bitterly that the laundry owner is one of those "guys who waltz through life dropping their socks behind them for other people to pick up. Am I destined to be a picker-upper?" (135).

Later, after Joanie has survived her ordeal and Bobby has returned her safely home, he revisits this thought: "Everything had worked out. What's so bad about being a picker-upper? Better than making messes, right? Shane was a picker-upper" (139). The important point here is that to "pick up" is to take both action *and* responsibility. Bobby has finally turned his back on movie fantasy, has accepted responsibility, and has taken credible, real-life action in support of his friend. He has survived that rite-of-passage experience better equipped to deal with his next, climactic challenge.

It begins when he returns to work the next day to see Fire Department volunteers carrying Lolly out of the plant on a stretcher. The inevitable has happened: the leaking steam pipe has ruptured, and Lolly has been badly burned. Once again the drivers do little but talk about the accident. For Diana, however, it is an imperative catalyst for action. When Bobby returns to the plant at mid-day after his morning route, he discovers that she has prepared a petition asking Sinclair to meet with a committee of employees to discuss the dangerous working conditions at the laundry. In a dramatic scene the drivers refuse to sign, and when Bump pleads with Diana to give up, she insists that she has to do something, adamantly adding, "I can't do nothing" (146).

When Axel, Diana's supervisor, threatens to fire her for insubordination if she presents the petition to Sinclair, it is Bobby's turn, once again, to act. He snatches the petition from Diana's hand and resolutely takes it inside to the plant owner. Sinclair's reaction is predictable: "Don't push me, Marks," he sneers. "This is real life, not the movies," and, tearing the petition into pieces, he drops them into Bobby's hand (147). When Bobby counters by telling Sinclair about Joanie's abortion, the owner takes the news "like a shot in the mouth" and Bobby feels momentarily triumphant, thinking, "A verbal knockout punch" (148).

Bobby's triumph is short-lived, however, for, like a veteran fighter, Sinclair rallies and delivers his own knockout punch. He fires Bobby on the spot, shrewdly reminding him of the reality of the circumstance: "You're the criminal here. Accessory to an abortion. There's no way you can tell anyone about me without implicating yourself in a felony" (148–49). Bobby's response shows how much he has learned about real-life heroism. Resisting the impulse to assault the older man, he returns to the yard and, vaulting to the top of a truck, rallies the workers.

"See this?" he shouts, tossing the confetti-like scraps of petition into the air, "that's what Roger Sinclair thinks of you" (150).

Sinclair himself appears in the doorway at this point and orders the employees back to work. But defiant Diana climbs up beside Bobby and urges the workers to stick together, wisely noting that their employer cannot fire all of them. Bobby presses their advantage, shouting to Sinclair that the employees will not return to work until all of the equipment has been repaired. When the now-energized workers roar their support, Sinclair bows to the inevitable and agrees to meet with an employee grievance committee once a month. But on one important condition: "That sonuvabitch goes," he snarls, pointing to Bobby (152).

Marks understands that he means it, and gracefully agrees. He then jumps, less gracefully, from the top of the truck, but no one notices; the workers are all too busy congratulating each other on their unexpected victory. So Bobby walks alone, in heroic, splendid isolation, to the gate. There he turns, and seeing that he is still unobserved, he thinks, wistfully, "If this was the movies, I would have been able to give a little speech, like Holden in *Stalag 17*" (153).

But there are to be no speeches, no little Brandon DeWilde character running heartbrokenly after him crying, "Come back Shane, come back, Bobby." As Bobby once again turns away from the yard, he figuratively turns away from the movie-fueled fantasies of his adolescence and walks, alone, into the reality of the adult life that awaits him. Like his former heroes, Bobby's own destiny may be in question, but there is now no doubt that he will greet it with vigor, a will to action, and a redeeming sense of humor.

The Summerboy has its flaws: the occasional problem of tone and its ancillary violation of the integrity of literary form being two we have already discussed. Additionally Roger Sinclair is a dangerously one-dimensional villain in his unqualified evilness. And there is some careless plotting: for example, Bobby discovers that Sinclair is Joanie's lover when he observes them kissing on a very public tennis court, and it is hard to believe that they would have been so indiscreet. But on the whole this title is a more rewardingly complex work than *Summer Rules* and, as the thematically richest of the three novels about Bobby Marks, a deeply satisfying conclusion to the trilogy.

Though not planned as such, the three books, in retrospect, have the coherence of one long novel, a bildungsroman[6] that introduces us to one of the most memorable characters in modern young adult literature. Though firmly rooted in a richly realized setting, in terms of both place and time, the problems and possibilities that visit Bobby's life are universal and timeless. Every adolescent must confront the possibilities of self-transformation, the pain and frustration of sexual awakening, the ordeal of feeling oneself an outsider, the need to establish ethical parameters for one's life, and the related need to deal with the sometimes painful realities of emerging adulthood.

Bobby is such a fully realized, multidimensional character that one can understand Lipsyte's own pain at saying good-bye to him, especially since, for the author, that must have been like saying good-bye all over again to his own personal adolescence. But say "good-bye" he did, and, what is more, following the 1982 publication of *The Summerboy*, he also once again said "Adios" to the entire field of young adult literature for another nine-year period.

8. TV Time

"In television the work is easy . . . but the life is very hard."

What lured Lipsyte away from young adult literature this time was the proverbial offer he could not refuse. As he wrote in the revised edition of *Assignment Sports*, "One morning in the spring of 1982, Shad Northshield and Bud Lamoreaux, the executive producers of the CBS 'Sunday Morning' show, asked me if I'd like to appear on television. It would mean hitting the road again and writing on deadline, learning a new field and meeting new people" (138).

Though Lipsyte does not specify it, this offer did not materialize out of the ether. He was already an established figure in broadcasting, having served as a radio commentator for National Public Radio since 1976. But, as a different medium, television was a new challenge that he gladly accepted, and for the next four years he worked as a television journalist for the prestigious news-magazine program. It is important to understand that as a "Sunday Morning" correspondent, Lipsyte was not doing play-by-play reports or providing "color" for game coverage. He was writing and broadcasting television essays, not unlike the columns he had earlier been writing for the *New York Times* or the radio pieces he had done for NPR. The very first piece he did for *Sunday Morning*, a profile of the former New York Giants linebacker Dan Lloyd, evidences this and is representative of the kinds of "electronic essays" he would do for the next four years, essays which proved that, for Lipsyte, it was still the player and not the game which mattered in sports.

The PBS television host, 1989. Lipsyte in the middle of a heated exchange between Bill Moyers and Brendan Gill about Joseph Campbell. Photo by Kate Kunz.

Dan Lloyd's football career had been interrupted at the age of twenty-seven when he was diagnosed as having cancer. Despite the long odds, he was determined to beat the beast and return to pro football. Though he accomplished the former, he had not yet succeeded at the latter, despite his singleminded determination, when Lipsyte's profile of him, "Wounded Winner," appeared on Sunday, 12 September 1982, the first Sunday of the regular 1982 National Football League season. "I was proud of the story, and glad that it was my debut," Lipsyte recalled later. "I just wish that it had a happier ending" (145; a training injury destroyed Lloyd's dream of returning to the Giants). Lipsyte's own successful fight against cancer, which had been diagnosed in the summer of 1978, no doubt sparked his interest in the story of the young linebacker and enhanced his empathy for Lloyd, whom Lipsyte recalled sitting next to in the outpatient clinic of New York's Memorial Sloan-Kettering Cancer Center, though he did not know who Lloyd was at the time.

In 1986 Lipsyte left CBS to become a correspondent for rival network NBC, filing stories for *NBC Nightly News* about such far-afield subjects as baseball in Nicaragua, another irresistible topic for Lipsyte, since it offered an opportunity to observe a national sport being played in the crucible of Sandanista versus Contra political turmoil (even the sports pages were subject to government censorship at the time).

Lipsyte was able to create some turmoil of his own when he left NBC in 1989 to accept what, for him, was a dream job: hosting his own public affairs program, "The Eleventh Hour," for PBS in New York. Television critic John Leonard praised the show, noting, "It's about time our public television station sat itself down in the middle of this imperial city in the years of the plague and did some raging." As for Lipsyte, Leonard hailed him as "opinionated, passionate, and a skin-bracing scourge." The critic seemed to take special delight in watching the host tear up, "with his bare hands," a paperback copy of Tom Wolfe's best-selling and locally controversial novel, *The Bonfire of the Vanities*. But he also rejoiced to see Lipsyte "take on" such diverse guests and topics as "crack dealers, real-estate developers, rats in Spanish Harlem, racial tensions between blacks and Koreans on 125th Street, the many hatreds of Mayor Ed Koch, and the decline of liberalism"—many of the same issues, in short, that had fired Lipsyte's imagination in *The Contender* and *Jock and Jill*. Leonard's final word about the show was "surprising," high praise coming from a jaded and sophisticated critic.[1] The show went on to win an Emmy Award, but, to Lipsyte's sorrow, it lasted only two seasons.

Looking back at his eight-year television career recently, Lipsyte continued to think fondly of *The Eleventh Hour*—"I loved that. That was great"—but admitted that he "didn't really enjoy most television." He explained why: "In television the work is easy. Very easy. But the life is very hard. I mean, you know, so much standing around, so much traveling, so much unnecessary stress, so many assholes in charge. And then worrying about—I mean, this is nothing [he points at his interviewer's tape recorder]. I mean, can you imagine sound *and* camera, doing stuff over and over again and then a f—ing cloud passes and your day is wiped out. It's terrible."

What he did enjoy about television and found helpful with his later writing in an experiential way was the unprecedented access TV gave him to people's lives. "You could get into people's lives in ways that were just amazing. Once they allowed you access—and I never understood why they would; I certainly wouldn't—you hung out with them, you saw everything and heard everything." Although "very little of this emerged on screen, as a learning experience, it was a great time." Though Lipsyte regretted the cancelation of his television show, the timing was, in a sense, fortuitous. It gave him an opportunity to resume writing a column for the *New York Times* at a period (the early nineties) when, as he put it, "I wanted to see how the world had changed—how I had changed. It was a terrific challenge."[2]

The Brave

Another "terrific challenge" was the opportunity to re-enter the world of young adult fiction. Since the mid-eighties, Lipsyte recalls, "I [had] wanted to write again. I wanted something new to say [and] I kept wondering when my own contender would show up on those stairs" ("Listening," 294). Finally, in 1987, one did. Visiting the Onondaga Reservation near Syracuse, New York, to cover a story, Lipsyte met a seventeen-year-old Native American boy who had run away to New York City for one night. Lipsyte explains that many young people, like this boy, feel trapped on the reservation. "It's a very dysfunctional society, as much as they would have you believe it's a real community. But if you leave, the young people are told, the white world is going to destroy you. So what do you do?"

Running away was not the final answer for the young man Lipsyte met. He was quickly picked up by the police in New York's Times Square, and, after a night at Covenant House, he was put on a bus back to the reservation the very next morning. Not the final answer, but it may have been a first step toward one, as Lipsyte points out: "I thought it would have been some sort of humiliation for him, but [instead] it was a hope. He was alive. He had done something. He was going to do it again someday. And maybe the next time he wouldn't come back." "Then I began wondering," Lipsyte added to another interviewer, "what would happen if a kid who could *really* box was stuck on this reservation? Where would he go? What if he ran away?"[3]

So Lipsyte had found another contender—but, as Alfred Brooks had been, a contender from another culture. Fortuitously, however, the author had also found another guide. Just as Dick Gregory had taught Lipsyte about African-American culture, so Oren Lyons would teach him about the Native American world. A former All-American lacrosse player and planning director for seasonal lines at Norcross Greeting Cards in New York, Lyons is a Native American faithkeeper—or adviser—to the chiefs of the Onondaga Nation. Lipsyte had met him at the same reservation where he met his "contender," though several years earlier while on assignment for *Sunday Morning*. Lipsyte muses, "Every so often you find somebody who just seems kind of wise and is not on a power trip, and if you allow him to, he will take you into another world where you will learn what the questions are." Lipsyte stresses this point: "There's no problem getting answers. You go around and ask."

But to him it is important to find "people [like Lyons] who will teach you what the *questions* are. And give you a beginning of an idea of what it means to be [Native American] in America. Over the years we became friends and I went back a lot, learned a lot about them [Native Americans], and spent a lot of time on the Reservation. And it turns out there *is* some other sensibility, some other . . . rule about them," which, Lipsyte believes, may remain forever fugitive to a white writer. Because of this, he explains, he "didn't really feel competent to do a full Indian character. And besides," he continues, "there are Indian writers to write about that."

What to do then? The answer was the creation of Sonny Bear, the hero of *The Brave* (1991), Lipsyte's long-awaited sequel to *The Contender*. Sonny is a seventeen-year-old mixed-blood boxer from the "Moscondaga" reservation. His mother is a Native American whose father was a chief, but *Sonny's* long-dead father was white, a soldier killed in Vietnam. *"That* was something I felt I could deal with," Lipsyte asserts, "the two aspects of his life: the Indian part and the white part and the struggle between the two."

Sonny is a classic outsider, a character who must try to live in two worlds but yet, because of his mixed blood, belongs in neither. The boxing ring may be the one place where he can truly belong. Yet the white men who control the only venues where an untested amateur like Sonny can get a bout—the Friday night smokers in mean-spirited small towns—are determined to cheat him of his victories in order to award them, instead, to the local (white) favorites. Sonny's challenge is not only to survive in the netherworld between the reservation and the ring but also to manage what he calls "the Monster," the rage against injustice that seethes inside him and that, unchecked, can destroy him. To Sonny's full-blooded great-uncle Jake, who doubles as his surrogate father and trainer, the monster is the Hawk Spirit of the Moscondaga Nation. "Find the Hawk inside you and let it loose and follow it," Jake counsels Sonny.[4]

Jake's grandfather, Sonny's great-great-grandfather, was the last of the legendary Running Braves, a near-mythical, select group of braves who served as diplomats, warriors, peace bringers, and couriers ready to run a hundred miles, if necessary, in service to the Nation. (Significantly, Lipsyte's guide, Oren Lyons, is "one of the leading courier/diplomats, or 'runners,' of the Native American world, a representative at many conferences, from Wounded Knee to Geneva."[5]) Though the white man has outlawed the runners, Jake has been taught their secrets by his grandfather and claims that Sonny is "the last one with the blood of the Running Braves" (13). Sonny cynically dismisses this as a fairy tale, an attitude consistent with his ambivalence about traditional Native American culture. For him the reservation is a place where he has been "dumped" by his peripatetic artist mother whenever money has run low or whenever her ambitions did not include being a mother. Like Oren Lyons, Sonny is a high-school dropout and, like Lyons, a talented artist, though, as Jake tells Alfred, nobody is supposed to know about that.

Blatantly cheated of one victory too many, Sonny finally resolves to give up boxing and go to New York City to find his mother and demand she sign his enlistment papers for the army (at seventeen he is still a minor). Jake's attitude about this is philosophical: "No man ever got to be a Running Brave without taking a dangerous journey. Maybe this is it for you" (19). The danger begins the moment Sonny steps off the bus in New York's Port Authority Terminal. He is picked up by a young black drug dealer named Stick and his girlfriend, the waiflike Doll, for whom Sonny feels an immediate physical attraction. Within fifteen minutes Sonny unwittingly fouls up a police drug bust and decks one of the arresting officers, allowing the target, Stick, to escape.

The police officer, of course, turns out to be Alfred Brooks—yes, *that* Alfred Brooks. The former contender is now a chunky, bearded, fortyish police sergeant who is obsessed with arresting the drug-dealing Stick. "Every time I think about Stick," he will tell Sonny, "I think about James" (81). Readers of *The Contender* will remember that James Mosely, Alfred's best friend when they were boys, was a heroin addict. Any reader, though, will understand Alfred's bitterness as he tells Sonny what later happened to his friend. Despite his struggle to get James clean, a struggle that went so far as enlisting in the army and fighting in Vietnam with him, Brooks explains that "they" (the Sticks of the world) were waiting for James's return to the streets, waiting like predators with the first free fix—all it took to once again hook James, who, scarcely a month later, was dead from a drug overdose.

Despite his bitterness, cynicism, and world-weariness, Brooks is intrigued by Sonny—because of his boxing skills, obviously, but also because of something Sonny unwittingly lets slip during Brooks's initial interrogation of him. When pressed to explain why he has left home, Sonny says, "Be somebody" (34). Brooks's reply is an understated "Everybody's somebody," but inside he must be feeling an overwhelming sense of déjà vu. For Sonny's statement precisely recalls Alfred's own statement to

Mr. Donatelli twenty years earlier. "I want to be somebody," he had told the man the first time he climbed the dark, winding stairs, alone, to the gym. "Everybody is somebody," had been Donatelli's own simple reply.

In a sense, Alfred sees himself in Sonny. But it would be a mistake to think that Alfred then releases Sonny from custody for the sake of sentimental nostalgia. Instead, it is cold-blooded calculation. Alfred gambles that Sonny will lead him to Stick. And he does—eventually. In a series of vividly realized, fast-paced chapters, Sonny is first duped by Stick into becoming a "mule," a drug delivery boy, and is then recaptured by Brooks and, when he refuses to cooperate in capturing Stick (for fear of jeopardizing Doll), is sent to a juvenile correctional facility. There he assaults a guard, is sent to solitary confinement, is released into the general prison population at Brooks's instigation, and when he refuses to affiliate with a prison gang, is knifed and nearly dies of the wound.

All of these incidents powerfully demonstrate that Sonny is unable to control the "Monster" inside of himself and that this failing seems almost to conspire with other external forces that also seek to control his life, to rob him of his will. Arrested for the second time, Sonny, we are told, "was helpless, a child again, his life out of his control" (60). In part, this is the price of his own stubbornness. But it is also an aspect of his Native American self, that part which is the opposite of what a former teammate told Lipsyte about Oren Lyons: "Oren was different from other Indian athletes. He was on time, he accepted discipline" ("Lacrosse," 68).

Sonny will *not* accept discipline. Brooks is quick to recognize this problem. He and Sonny watch a boxing match on television while the latter is in the hospital recovering from his knife wound. "You think those guys are better than you?" Brooks suddenly asks.

"No," Sonny replies. "Wrong," Brooks declares. "You might have a better punch, you might even be quicker and smarter and stronger, but they got off their butts and did it . . . they got control of themselves" (82). Sonny's simple reply, "I could try," is terribly significant, since it is the first evidence that he may be willing to undergo the same demanding experience that both Brooks as a boy and Bobby Marks did: that of self-transformation. The agents for this change are the same for all three protagonists: punishingly hard work and steely self-control. Just as Alfred had an ally in Mr. Donatelli when he undertook this process, so Sonny will have a similar ally, now, in Alfred, who has a plan.

It is simple and sensible, calling for Sonny, on his release from the hospital, first to return to the reservation, where Jake will work with him to get him back into shape, and then to go to the city to work out at Donatelli's Gym. The contrast between the two training methods extends the theme of duality that is symbolized by Sonny's mixed blood. "You got the worst of both sides," Jake growls. "The white side thinks you're too good to work hard, and the Indian side thinks you're not good enough to make it" (93). (Lyons had earlier told Lipsyte that Indians routinely "expect rejection.")

Jake's approach, accordingly, is to give the boy the *best* of both sides: to train Sonny as if he were becoming not only a disciplined boxer but also a dedicated Running Brave. Jake teaches Sonny the stick dance, kicking a twig from foot to foot: "Balance. Footwork. Concentration. First things a Running Brave learns" (87). He teaches him the importance of position, of misdirection, of breathing through his nose, of listening and thinking. And all the while he tells him stories about his grandfather and the deeds of the Running Braves.

If Brooks has a plan, so does the far-sighted Jake: he shows Sonny the sign of the Running Braves, pushing his thumb between his third and fourth fingers and curling his hand into a fist, and explains, "It's a secret." " 'So why are you showing me . . . ' Sonny stopped. He felt suddenly chilled. . . . 'There's gonna be big troubles here someday,' said Jake [speaking of the reservation]. 'White man's gonna figure out he can use this raggedy place. For gambling maybe. . . . Chiefs ain't strong enough to hold the Nation together. The People gonna need a Brave'" (102–3). That Brave, according to Jake's plan, will be Sonny.

It is at this portentous moment that Sonny's mother arrives in a stretch limousine with her new boyfriend, who operates a string of luxury hotels in the lobbies of which the two plan to open "authentic" Indian shops called "Sweet Bear's Kiva." "'Authentic.' Jake rolled his eyes. 'Kiva is not in our language'" (105). Sonny's mother sidesteps the issue of having sold out her Indian heritage and grandly announces that she has come to collect Sonny so that he can work in the shops with her. When Sonny replies that he wants to stay with Jake and train to be a fighter, instead, his mother's angry reply is directed to Jake not to her son: "Sonny's got a chance to be somebody now. I'm not going to let you spoil it" (106).

The irony here is that Sonny, for the first time, *does* have a chance to be somebody—a boxer and a savior of his people. But to his mother "being somebody" means betraying one's heritage or bastardizing it for commercial purposes. There is no question that she could now offer Sonny financial security for the first time in his life, and, in that sense, she is a temptress in much the same way as Doll, who would seduce Sonny into being a minion of Stick's. It is no wonder that in his dreams and imaginings Sonny often confuses Doll's face with his mother's.

With Jake's help, however, Sonny escapes from his mother, who has threatened to call the sheriff, and heads, alone, for New York. It is nearly midnight when he arrives at 125th Street and Seventh Avenue in Harlem. Anyone who has read *The Contender* will be powerfully moved as the solitary Sonny climbs the dark, narrow, twisting steps, just as Alfred had done twenty years before and finds, at the top, not Mr. Donatelli (now long dead) but Brooks himself. And this time it is Brooks not Donatelli who explains what a contender is: "A guy coming up, willing to bust his tail and take his lumps to find out just how far he can go." As for what Jake calls "the spirit and the Hawk" (and what Sonny calls "the Monster"): "Mr. Donatelli believed there was a fire inside. . . . Fear is that fire. The great champions use that fear— they turn it into fury when they need it. You learn to do that, you can beat anything, anywhere" (111).

Sonny's mission, as well as the book's theme, is now clear: through the rigors of training to learn to control the spirit/ hawk/monster/fear/fire; to use it and even to release it so that it can show him the way to his destiny. Quoting these various expressions of theme out of context may make it appear that *The Brave* is narrowly didactic or artless in its expression of theme. In fact, the contrary is true. One of the most satisfying aspects of this book is how artfully the author has planted the seeds of his themes and then permitted them to grow organically from incident, which is always a function or expression of the personality of his carefully realized characters, or from natural and realistic dialogue. As an example of the art of the novel, *The Brave* is, arguably, the best of Lipsyte's works.

To pay for the use of the gym, Sonny goes to work for Henry Johnson, who now owns Donatelli's (in *The Contender* Henry was a teenager who worked at the gym and served as Alfred's second). Sonny's assigned training partner is a young African-American named Martin Witherspoon, who is the son of Bill Witherspoon, Alfred's hero in *The Contender* and now a middle-aged school principal. In a neat twist Martin, though at first indifferent, will make Sonny *his* hero when Jake shows up unannounced and the impressionable young man realizes, for the first time, that Sonny is a Native American and not just a "wiseguy with a pony tail" (125).

It turns out that Martin is a would-be writer who dreams of going to the reservation to interview Jake and who promises Sonny that he will write a book about him when he becomes champ, a promise he will make good as the putative author of the sequel to *The Brave*, *The Chief*. Meanwhile Sonny is bemused by Martin's hero worship and annoyed when Jake (who never misses an opportunity) points out that every Running Brave had a young warrior-in-training. For the time being it is Sonny who is the warrior-in-training, however, rising every morning before dawn to run in Central Park, just as Alfred had done, practicing combinations, shadowboxing, exercising—undergoing all the rites of passage for a beginning boxer. There is the first match with a sparring partner (Sonny wins, of course), the first prefight meal at the Witherspoons', where Alfred had always eaten when he was a boxer; there are five fights, each one a learning experience, each one getting him closer to the Gotham Gloves finals, where he will be matched against Elston Hubbard, Jr., the son of the boxer who had beaten Alfred in his last fight twenty years earlier. Hubbard Senior is now a TV actor and a born promoter. "My boy versus Alfred's boy," he crows for the cameras, "the continuation of a quarter-century grudge match." Then, adding sotto voce to Sonny, "Never pass up publicity." "Brooks winked at Sonny. He looked proud and happy" (164–65).

Less than a week later, the very day of the Gotham Gloves final match, Alfred, no longer "proud and happy," will instead be lying in a hospital bed, paralyzed and near death from a line-of-duty gunshot wound to the back. His assailant has been Stick, but, as we will soon learn, Sonny is the only one who has deduced that. Though Alfred manages to rally long enough to urge Sonny to win, there is more bad news to come: Sonny arrives at the boxing arena only to learn that he has been disqualified. Someone has told the Boxing Commission about his six "pro" fights—the upstate smoker bouts. Though seemingly inconsequential, these destroy his amateur status because he has been paid for the fights. Sonny's disqualification is a case of art imitating life, for he is, of course, not the first Native American to suffer such a fate. Jim Thorpe, perhaps the greatest athlete of the twentieth century, was stripped of his amateur status and his Olympic medals in 1913 when it was discovered that he had played semi-pro baseball. Even earlier—in 1880—Native American lacrosse teams "were judged professionals because they allegedly took money to play. They were excluded from the Canadian championships . . . and soon afterward from all international competition" ("Lacrosse," 61).

Lipsyte deals with the Thorpe case at some length in his recent biography of the Native American athlete (*Jim Thorpe: 20th Century Jock*, 1993), particularly the issue of whether justice was served: "Jim had never tried to be dishonest, yet he became a scapegoat for a system that was itself dishonest." Sonny's own culpability or innocence is less clear-cut. When Henry protests that he should have been told of the earlier bouts, Sonny's reply is a simple, perhaps disingenuous, "Didn't think of it" (176). The system itself is no shining example of integrity, of course, but this alone would not excuse Sonny from the reader's censure if he had knowingly hidden the fact of the "pro" fights. Most, however, will probably presume that Sonny, like Thorpe before him, "never tried to be dishonest."

In any event the more important issue is that the two blows, coming in such rapid succession, serve as a catalyst to action for Sonny. With Martin in tow, he drives Jake's old truck to Times Square, where he confronts Stick in the latter's underground hideout. Holding Sonny at bay with a shotgun, Stick asks, "What do you want?" Sonny's reply is a chillingly terse "Come to kill you" (180). Stick rightly presumes that Sonny plans to avenge Brooks and says, "It was him or me," unwittingly admitting his guilt.

Sonny then cleverly employs misdirection, a tactic he has learned from Jake, feigning disinterest in Brooks and demanding to know, instead, why Stick has turned him in to the Commission. Stick is bewildered, claiming—truthfully—that he does not know what Sonny is talking about. (In fact, it is Sonny's mother who has been the snitch.) Sonny pretends to be defeated, and a relieved Stick drops his guard. Sonny then makes his move, disarming Stick and pointing Jake's old pistol at him: "'Now I'm going to kill you.' Sonny felt the wings rustling inside his chest. Yes" (183). Thus begins the most important fight of his life—not with Stick, but with the monster that demands, "Kill him for Brooks."

For Sonny it is an agonizing struggle and one that recalls every lesson Jake and Brooks have tried to teach him about the importance of control and the wisdom of the Running Braves. "A Running Brave would know what to do," he thinks desperately. "He would have remembered everything he learned on his journey . . . and make the right decision for the People" (184–85). Suddenly Sonny knows what to do: he must not kill Stick but, instead, he must turn him in to the police. Having finally taken control of himself and the situation, Sonny feels a great sense of catharsis and realizes that he has set the Hawk free. And in so doing he has set himself free, as well, to finally follow his own destiny.

The book ends with Sonny rededicated to boxing, to becoming a champ the hard way: turning pro for real and fighting his way to the top via small clubs, fighting in tank towns for bad pay in worse conditions, beginning in the Hillcrest lodge hall where he had been cheated out of a victory at the very outset of the book. This time, however, he wins and, savoring the victory, thinks, "It was going to get harder now. But he was going to make it" (194). Just as Alfred Brooks had twenty years before, Sonny has become a contender, a man "who's willing to sweat and bleed to get up as high as his legs and his brains and his heart will take him."

Lipsyte's belief in the importance of this willingness to bleed might seem to contradict his earlier condemnation of athletes being encouraged to compete when they are injured, but only if you interpret "bleed" literally; I believe Lipsyte means it symbolically. For him, to "bleed" means to embrace the necessity for punishingly hard work and spartan self-sacrifice to attain one's goal.

9. Metafiction Man

"A wordslinger between books and marriages."

Anxious readers did not have to wait long to learn just how hard and high Sonny's climb would be. Less than two years after the publication of *The Brave*, a sequel, *The Chief*, appeared. In the novel's internal chronology two years have also passed. Alfred Brooks, now a paraplegic confined to a wheelchair as a result of the gunshot wound, is managing Sonny's boxing career. Uncle Jake is still talking about what the increasingly bitter Sonny cynically calls "the redskin crap." Martin, now nineteen like Sonny, is a college student but is still serving part-time as Sonny's "third second," is still writing, and is still dreaming of being a contender himself in the "ring" of creative writing. Sonny, less sanguine about his own future, is depressed by the fact that Elston Hubbard, Jr., whom he was to have fought for the Gotham Gloves title before being disqualified, is now in Las Vegas for a shot at the championship title, while he is still fighting in bush-league venues behind abandoned factories. In fact, Sonny has begun using the word "futile" to describe his boxing career, and Martin thinks his friend might be ready to "dump the dream."[1]

Indeed, when Sonny is cheated of yet another victory (a prejudiced referee declares that Sonny is too badly injured to continue and so awards the decision to his opponent on a technical knockout), he returns to the reservation and announces that he is quitting boxing and flying to Phoenix to finally work with his mother in her chain of "authentic" Indian craft boutiques, "Sweet Bear's Kiva," where he will sell crafts designed by her but manufactured in Singapore and Korea. Summoned to the reservation by Jake the night before Sonny's scheduled departure, Martin realizes that "there was still a chance to get to him. He hadn't made up his mind yet" (53). Martin cannily presses this advantage and persuades Sonny to fly to Las Vegas to do "the Muhammad Ali number" (58). This is a reference to Ali's strategy, early in his career, of making so much noise in the media that important opponents literally had to fight him. The idea of following Ali's example is not original with Martin. It has been suggested earlier by a young woman named Robin Bell who is producing a television documentary about boxing. According to Bell, "You've got to make your own publicity and connections." "If you get off your butt, you'll make it," she then challenges Sonny, "because in your heart you really want it" (26, 28).

She's right, of course, and the reader is not surprised when Sonny finally allows Martin to persuade him to fly to Las Vegas. Once there, the combination of Marty's bravado and Sonny's unconventional background capture the attention of the media, and, in due course, Sonny once again finds himself a viable contender booked for a match with Junior Hubbard. For professional boxing is, indeed, as Lipsyte is at pains to demonstrate, "all publicity and connections."

The Chief is a much less traditional coming-of-age novel than its predecessor, *The Brave*, and in some ways a more interesting one, since Lipsyte has dared this time to write in Martin's brash and breezy first-person voice. The author's interesting conceit here is that *The Chief* is a work-in-progress by the young would-be writer. As we discover in the fifth chapter, Martin is submitting the first four chapters to win approval from his new writing professor for a semester of independent study. This will give him the necessary freedom to travel with Sonny and finish writing the book.

Martin is not the first of Lipsyte's characters to aspire to publish, of course. Bobby Marks is also a would-be writer, but the difference between him and Martin is that we actually get to read Martin's work. And also, Bobby tells his own story, while Martin is telling Sonny's, as a participant in the action, to be sure, but also as observer and commentator on the same action. Interestingly,

Lipsyte finds a way to interject his own commentary—as Martin's creator—on Martin's work-in-progress. To do this he reintroduces his alter ego, Bobby Marks, as a character. Bobby is now a professional writer in his mid-fifties, "a wordslinger between books and marriages," as he sardonically puts it (33). (Lipsyte was himself between marriages when this was written, his second marriage, with novelist Marjorie Rubin, having ended in 1987.) With no new books in the offing, Bobby has now become "Professor" Marks, head of the university's writing program. (In the early and mid-1970s Lipsyte also taught writing—nonfiction and journalism—at Fairleigh Dickinson and New York University, respectively.) Of course, Bobby does not describe his circumstances so prosaically. Instead, he grandly tells Martin, "I'm here to goose up the program and then ride into the sunset before anyone can shoot back" (33). (The adult Marks obviously still finds his imagery in the western movies of his adolescence.)

The central conceit—that the book is being written by one of its characters, who mentally agonizes over its progress—and the related introduction of Marks as a character to offer his own commentary and criticism on the work-in-progress clearly establish *The Chief* as a work of metafiction (fiction that is self-consciously aware of its existence as fiction), a form that playfully blurs the line between imagination and reality. This form is interesting in its own right, but it also works nicely to enhance one of the book's ambitious themes: the interrelationship and occasional confusion of illusion and reality. This theme has interested Lipsyte since the autobiographical Bobby Marks trilogy (it is no accident that Bobby, in *Summer Rules*, invokes the name of the Italian playwright Luigi Pirandello, whose most famous work, *Six Characters in Search of an Author*, deals with this same theme).

Lipsyte's theme will emerge in an intriguing variety of ways in the book: in the media's misrepresentation and distortion of reality as they labor to manufacture a new identity for Sonny; in Sonny's subsequent journey to the fantasy world of Hollywood, where he is "discovered" as a potential "property"; in the odd nature of producer Robin Bell's television version of reality, which is quite different from Martin's writerly version; in the "fairy tale" beliefs of Jake about the Moscondaga past; in Sonny's mother's "authentic" Indian crafts; and so on. It is also present in such small details as the fact that Marks's agent, Theron, is modeled after Lipsyte's own real-life agent, Theron Raines, and that a rock band called "Dung Beetle" that plays a peripheral role in the book is, in reality, the band of Lipsyte's son Sam, who is a rock musician.

But the book's clearest exposition of the blurred symbiosis of illusion and reality is in the author's treatment and use of character, principally his introduction of himself as a character in the guise of the now-adult Bobby Marks. But it is even more complex than that, involving what Lipsyte referred to in an interview as the "psychosis that is writing. You begin to think that some of your characters really lived" (Ruby, 146). What this means to him was demonstrated in one of the most interesting of the monthly columns he is currently writing for *American Health* magazine. Titled "The Five-Mile Run," it reports Lipsyte's stubborn determination to complete a mini-marathon.

> By the time I passed 3¹/₂ miles, I realized the enormity of my mistake. I wasn't going to make it. I heard footsteps beside me and I sensed another runner. A voice said, "C'mon, whitey, you can do it."
>
> It was Alfred Brooks . . . from *The Contender*. He was running beside me. I saw him.
>
> "I made you up," I said.
>
> "You made me up for *this*," he said.
>
> Then I felt the presence of a runner on my other side.
>
> "C'mon, fatty, pick it up." It was Bobby Marks from *One Fat Summer* . . . who lost 40 pounds pushing a lawn mower.
>
> "You can't run at all," I said.
>
> "Maybe not in *your* book," he said.
>
> And then two big guys—Jack Ryder . . . and Sonny Bear . . . ran ahead of me to clear the way.
>
> I ran the last mile blind. I don't know why I wasn't hit by a car . . . unless it was because Freddy Bauer [from *The Chemo Kid*] was up ahead of me stopping traffic and yelling, "C'mon, Lippy, you're the writer, you can pick any ending you want."

Lipsyte concludes the column by claiming the story is true, although he admits "as I tell it now, I find it very hard to believe."[2]

This is a good writer's story, of course, but anyone who remembers Bobby Marks's identical visitation in *One Fat Summer* by Big Bob Marks, Commander Marks, and Captain Marks, characters of *his* own creation, will have a pretty good idea of the source of this column and will understand that its "reality" is also metafictional. There is no question that Lipsyte's characters are very real to him personally, however. One reason for this may be that he spends an enormous amount of time on their creation, starting with their names: "I spend a lot of time on names. I do them based on figuring out when the character was born, who his parents were, and what they would have been thinking about at the time, so I always think that my names are very 'historical.'" The reader doesn't have to search far for examples of this: Sonny Bear's real name is George Harrison Bayer, the "George Harrison" being an homage to his mother's favorite Beatle. Similarly, Martin has been named by his parents in honor of Martin Luther King; he is the one who adds the "Malcolm," for "Malcolm X."

"Long before I start writing," Lipsyte continues, "I make a lot of notes about the characters, their families, where they're from, what was going on when they were growing up, how they got their names—things that do not necessarily appear in the book. (I have Robin Bell, the TV producer's resume somewhere, for example.) Then I try to put them [the characters] in situations. For example, when I was creating Sonny Bear, I wrote a lot of his experiences when he left the Reservation and went to high school in a local area. How he was treated. What happened when he played on teams. Just vignettes and little short stories which would never be in the book. So that by the time I get going, I have a really good idea who these people are. I have internalized their problems . . . so that everything that happens [in the resulting book] seems to evolve out of the character."

Lipsyte says that he purposely avoids overdescribing physical characteristics, however, preferring to leave that to the reader's imagination—unless the character's physicality is important to defining character and advancing action: as a heavyweight boxer, Sonny's physical person is important, so Lipsyte tells us specifically that he is six-foot-one and weighs 180–185 pounds. He has long black hair that he wears in a ponytail, which is emblematic of his being a Native American. He is also quite handsome, a fact that is necessary to attract the attention of the media and Hollywood in *The Chief*.

As a writer, Martin's physical person is less important and is, therefore, less specifically described, although we do know that he wears little round glasses and that he is fat (Sonny thinks of him as a fat black owl). Though not as completely described in physical terms as Sonny, Martin is clearly the more fully realized *character*. Lipsyte himself recognized this from the moment he introduced Martin halfway through *The Brave*. "It was a real struggle to keep him from taking over the book," he recalls, "because he's certainly much more verbal and powerful a character than Sonny."

The author's decision to tell Sonny's continuing story in *The Chief* through Martin's eyes and voice was, in part, a product of the fact that "Martin just had to have his own book!" But it was also due to Lipsyte's realization that "Sonny can't tell his story as well as Martin can. Sonny is a true hero. He's a man of action. He's not going to sit around and think about 'it.' He's going to do 'it.' Martin will make speculations about how Sonny feels about something that I think are probably truer than anything Sonny can [express]."

To allow Martin to tell Sonny's story, however, to let his consciousness be the filter through which Sonny's experiences will pass to the reader, means giving Martin, an urban black teenager, his own first-person voice. And inevitably this means reviving the delicate—and this time double-barreled—question of the voice's authenticity and authority. In short, should Lipsyte be "permitted" to write in the first-person voice of an African-American and should that character then be permitted to write about the life, external and internal, not of another African-American but of a Native American?

Lipsyte chooses to handle this complex question ironically by having "Professor" Marks—a middle-aged white man who is clearly Lipsyte himself—address it. Marks/Lipsyte criticizes Martin's original manuscript for not being "in the voice of a nine-teen-year-old urban Black male." Instead, Marks taunts, "You're writing dead white male. Witherspoon does Hemingway." Martin's immediate reply to Marks clearly represents Lipsyte's own point of view: "I hope, Professor Marks, you're not saying that because I'm Black I can only write about the Black *thang*" (30, 33). This is a neat reversal of the criticism that was leveled at Lipsyte, as a white man, for writing, in *The Contender*, about a black character. But, of course, the well-educated, middle-class Marty is quite a different black character than Alfred Brooks was.

In fact, Marty, like Sonny, falls somewhere between two worlds. For example on the train home from school after receiving Marks's stinging criticism, Marty notices that both the white con-ductor and a group of "gang-banger-wanna-bes" are eyeing him suspiciously. Angrily he realizes he is too black for the former and not black enough for either the latter or for his professor. Still angry when he arrives home, Marty complains to his parents that his white teacher is telling him his book is not black enough.

In fact, that is only part of what Marks/Lipsyte is criticizing. Though in the "real" world where the reader exists *The Chief* is a work of fiction, in the imagined world of the book it is a work of nonfiction, an exercise in Marty's reportage. "The information in your story is excellent," the teacher tells Marty, referring to the first four chapters. "It reeks with the credibility of journalism. This is NOT a course in journalism" (31). What is needed, Marks goes on to explain to the doubting Martin, is more of himself, of his own feelings, of his reactions. In other words Marty needs to make *himself* more of a character in his own book.

What Tracy Kidder, author of such acclaimed works of nonfic-tion as *The Soul of a New Machine, House,* and *Among School-children,* recently wrote of his own early career is relevant to this issue: "When I started writing nonfiction . . . I decided that writ-ers of nonfiction had a moral obligation to write in the first person . . . making themselves characters on the page. . . .

I would not hide the truth from the reader. . . . In retrospect it seems clear that . . . I was too young and self-absorbed to realize what should have been obvious: that I was less likely to write honestly about myself than about anyone else on earth."[3] Marty is mature enough to recognize this problem, however. Midway through the book, he pauses to reflect on what he has written thus far (more metafiction): "I thought I was emerging as a character in my own book. Marks was right about that being necessary" (120).

Another necessary part of Marty's attempt to get it "just right" will be his struggle to understand precisely who he and Sonny are. Still thinking about his work in progress, he wonders if he should have tried to transform a cut above Sonny's eye into a symbol "for his tragic flaw." Then, more realistically, he thinks, "What was Sonny's tragic flaw, other than he didn't know who he was yet?" (120).

For Robin Bell and Marty and even for Alfred it is important that Sonny's true identity turn out to be that of the youngest heavyweight champ in history. For Jake it is more important that Sonny's identity be that of a Running Brave so that he can save the Moscondaga Nation, which is now fragmented and polarized by a debate over whether a gambling casino should be built on the reservation grounds. Sonny's quest to discover who he should be is, of course, the book's central narrative consideration, and whether he will have the strength, the *will*, to define himself or will listlessly permit others to define him according to their needs provides the dramatic tension that drives the plot. Since Martin is not only an objective reporter of Sonny's progress but, as a character, an active participant as well, it is important that he also be engaged in a quest for self-discovery and self-definition. At first he, too, is in danger of being defined by others—Professor Marks or, more importantly, Sonny. After all, in *The Brave* and in the first chapters of *The Chief* Marty customarily identifies himself simply as "Sonny's writer." When Professor Marks turns down his request for independent study, Marty's reaction confirms that he finds his identity and professional future in Sonny: "It [his career as a writer] was over for me," he glumly thinks (125).

Meanwhile Sonny is having his own continuing identity crisis. Losing the fight with Hubbard on a TKO (a technical knockout), he accepts an offer to fly to Hollywood to discuss starring in a TV series that will offer a typically distorted view of the reality of being a Native American. Recognizing this but unable to articulate his point of view, Sonny finally sends for Martin, who is on a holiday break from college but still not writing, to come to Hollywood to be his spokesperson with the people who are developing the series. Sonny speaks for himself on TV talk shows, however, where he has become a fixture ("Sonny Hollywood," Jake snorts contemptuously) and willingly accepts the seductive temptations Hollywood offers the newly famous: drink, drugs, and indiscriminate sex. Marty begs him to come home to resume his boxing career, but Sonny angrily refuses: "Maybe I just don't want to get punched around anymore for nothing" (169).

That night Sonny goes off to yet another Hollywood party and Marty remains in the hotel, struggling to decide what to do. On the one hand he knows that Sonny needs him but on the other he has his own life to consider. Musing about this, he suddenly understands the meaning of something Alfred has told him earlier: "I could only be a friend to Sonny if I wasn't dependent on him, if it didn't matter what he did because I was strong in what I did. I didn't need for him to box for me to write. And we both had to come back off the floor" (170). It will require something more powerful than this kind of epiphany to get the less introspective Sonny "off the floor," however. As it happens, that something arrives the very next morning in the form of the disturbing news that Jake, whose stubborn traditionalism continues to threaten the construction of the casino, has been shot.

Marty pours the still-drunk Sonny onto a plane, and they fly back to New York. After stopping to see the now-recovering Jake in the hospital, Sonny and Marty then try to visit the governor to ask him to use his influence to stop the troubles at the reservation (shades of *Jock and Jill*). The governor's refusal to see them is the catalyst Sonny needs to act on his own behalf and, in the spirit of the Running Braves, on behalf of his Nation as well. Sonny announces that "to wake people up" he will run the three hundred miles from Manhattan to the reservation. "'Three hundred [miles],' said Sonny. 'Nothing for a Running Brave'" (185).

Sonny's dramatic run excites enormous media attention and, inevitably, that of Elston Hubbard, Sr., who shows up halfway to the reservation with an offer to arrange a match between Sonny and Floyd (The Wall) Hall, the reigning heavyweight champion. The match will be held, he dramatically announces, at the grand opening of the new casino on the Moscondaga reservation. Finally arriving at the reservation, Sonny, as "a Running Brave with a message for the Nation," dramatically calls for a meeting of the chief, the council of elders, the subchiefs, and the clan mothers to discuss the casino and whether he should fight there. The chief of chiefs accepts Sonny's call; his public pronouncement that Sonny will join them in the longhouse conference confirms Sonny's now undisputed identity as a Running Brave, as a member of the Moscondaga Nation, and as the grandson of a chief. It is ultimately decided that the hotel and casino will be allowed to operate and the match to be held, after a contract is signed making the Nation a partner and offering jobs to all the Moscondagas who want them. The book ends with Sonny entering the arena for his championship fight: "He had run and he had spoken and now it was time for the Running Brave to fight" (225).

Sonny has not only become a Running Brave, he has become a contender. He has once again climbed his climb. As for the fight? Marty may breathlessly predict that he is going to win, but it is, appropriately, Alfred Brooks, the original contender, who has the final word: "He already won, Marty. This is just the fight" (226). Marty, of course, has also won. In the locker room prior to the championship fight Sonny solemnly pronounces him a "Writing Brave." Together the two friends have finally found their true identities, and they are one and the same. Lipsyte has observed that the point of *The Chief* "is that these two guys are both trying to get into the rankings; they are both doing the same thing. I think that a writer is every bit as brave and risk-taking as an athlete is. They are just using different things. The athlete is using his body, basically, and his mind. The writer is using his mind . . . and his soul."

On a first reading, *The Chief* may seem a less realistic novel than *The Brave*. In part this is due to its satirical treatment of the press and media, the circuslike atmosphere of the scenes in Las Vegas, and the ironic revelation of Hollywood's rejection of reality (and integrity) for commercial gain. But there is truth in these depictions, and championship boxing does have an unreal quality, especially when compared to the worlds of amateur boxing and of the gritty, sweaty lower-echelon professional bouts described in *The Brave*.

Though it might be lost on the boxing promoters themselves, there is something nicely symbolic about the fact that many big-stakes bouts are held in Las Vegas and that it is here in this glitzy, unreal, nighttown world that Sonny gets his first big break. The frenzied, hyperbolic publicity and the cynical distortions and misrepresentations of the media, which Lipsyte so successfully satirizes, also lend an air of unreality, even of fantasy, to parts of *The Chief*. Outside the ring, however, the book is firmly rooted in reality. This often manifests itself in reports of the wincingly unpleasant details of Alfred's deteriorating physical condition. At one point, for example, he is in the hospital being treated for a chronic bowel infection. And when Marty and Sonny visit him, Alfred futilely tries to hide the feeding tube in his stomach and the urinary catheter between his legs. Another time Alfred disappears into the bathroom. And Marty reports, "He'll be gone for a while. After a long, tough day the tubes and plastic bags that catch his wastes could be backed up, or at least tangled" (25).

When asked if some of these details might be better left to the reader's imagination, Lipsyte bristles: "Leave it to whose imagination? To the imagination of a twelve-year-old in Iowa who may not even know a person in a wheelchair? It's a fact of Alfred's life. It becomes a fact of Martin's, too, when they're traveling together. How could you understand his [Alfred's] anger and bitterness and feelings, if you didn't have some sense of what he goes through? I mean, a guy gets shot in the back, his spine is severed, and everything is okay? He's in a lot of pain; he's got a lot of problems. How could you not write about it?" It is inar-

guably true that the reader becomes as emotionally involved with
Alfred's pain and frustration as Marty does.

Accordingly one of the most gratifying moments in the book
arrives with Alfred's excitement and high good humor at being
involved, at being *needed*, when Sonny makes the run from Manhattan to the reservation. Picking up Marty in his HandiVan,
Alfred grins and exultantly says, "Got my spare bladder bag, the
shotgun and the thirty-eight. Let's rock 'n' roll, little brother"
(189). Equally rooted in reality is the premise of constructing a
gambling casino on an Indian reservation. Indeed, this is becoming such a widespread phenomenon that the *Los Angeles Times*
reported, on 4 May 1993, that Atlantic City casino owner and
entrepreneur Donald Trump was actually suing Interior
Secretary Bruce Babbitt and the chairman of the National Indian
Gaming Commission, claiming, according to the *Times*, that
"Indian tribes are given preferential treatment in the granting of
casino licenses."[4]

And on 18 July 1993 the *New York Times* reported the impending opening on the Oneida reservation in central New York State
of the state's first legal casino in a century. What the *Times* said
of the Oneida situation describes, perfectly, that of the fictional
Moscondaga: "Until just a year ago, the Oneida Indians were in a
struggle against extinction. Their once-sprawling territory in
central New York had been whittled to a 32-acre grassy patch
where two dozen families lived in rusted trailer homes discarded
by the Federal government. Unemployment routinely topped
sixty percent. Their once-proud culture had been forgotten by
almost all but the elders."[5] Also reality-based is the tradition of
Running Braves, whose historical origins can be dated to as early
as 1680 when runners carried messages coded into carved sticks
and knotted strings to foment rebellion among Pueblo Indians
against Spanish colonists. The tradition remains alive in Sonny's
transformation.

Like all of Lipsyte's work, both *The Brave* and *The Chief* are
marvels of verisimilitude, thanks to the author's experiences of
the real world of the boxing arena, television, Hollywood, and the
reservation and also to his reporter's capacity to recall and

invoke the telling and the memorable detail. And thanks, as well, to his novelist's capacity to imagine credible characters whose choices and actions provide the dramatic incidents that, together, support the framework of narrative structure.

Will there be another novel about Sonny, Martin, Alfred, and the others? As this is being written in the early fall of 1993, Lipsyte is already thinking about one, to be titled (what else?) *The Champion*.

Film at eleven. . . .

10. Battling the Beast

"There was no evidence of cancer."

In the summer of 1978, Lipsyte was diagnosed with testicular cancer. As he wrote in the revised edition of *Assignment Sports*, "Like most people, we [he and his family] regarded cancer as one of the most dread words in the language; if not a death sentence, we thought, at least it meant the end of a normal, productive life. We knew very little about cancer, but we learned quickly. After surgery, I underwent two years of chemotherapy. I was sick for a day or two after each treatment, and I lost some strength and some hair, but we were amazed at how normally my life continued: I wrote, I traveled, I swam and ran and played tennis. After the treatments were over, my strength and my hair returned. There was no evidence of cancer" (138).

Until 1991, that is, when a second case of testicular cancer was diagnosed. "I was older," Lipsyte reflected in his *American Health* magazine column, "And this time I would do what I hadn't done the first time—I would write about it. In fact, this would be my breakthrough book, the Big One. I would be the first man to write an honest book about cancer the second time around, a cancer whose treatment would cause me to reevaluate the meaning of manhood. I had a title: *Coming Back Again*."[1]

Ultimately a book did emerge from Lipsyte's second bout with cancer. But it was not *Coming Back Again*. Instead, it was *The Chemo Kid* (1992), a novel in which Lipsyte came back again to young adult fiction.

Fred Bauer, *The Chemo Kid*'s eponymous hero, is an anonymous, unremarkable high school junior when we first meet him.

"You know what they'll write about Fred in the yearbook?" another student cruelly asks. "He was here. We think" (7).

Fred's de facto status as the invisible boy ends the night of the Junior Prom when his girlfriend, Mara, discovers a lump on his neck. It is a cancerous tumor, and to say that its discovery changes Fred's life is an understatement. For, following surgery, Fred is put on a course of experimental hormone treatments that invest him with superpowers, and he becomes the self-styled "Chemo Kid," a superhero powerful enough not only to defeat cancer but also to best the book's drug-dealing and environment-polluting villains, as well.

Ultimately, Lipsyte believes, *The Chemo Kid* is about "surviving cancer on your own terms." He explains: "In most books about kids with cancer, they die at the end . . . [but] the point [of this book] is not to find gallant ways to die with cancer; the point is to live with it." And, obviously, to survive it.

The novel's central conceit—the startling idea that treatments for cancer can give a patient superpowers—is grounded in Lipsyte's own first experience with cancer (which, in conversation, he calls "The Beast"). "My son Sam was ten when I had my first bout with the beast and he was very troubled. So, to bolster his spirits—and mine—I created this character called "Captain Cancer" who had superpowers, and it got us over the hump." (Ironically when Fred is thinking about names for his superpower-self, he briskly discards "Captain Cancer" as an option: "Sounds like he spreads it!" Fred snorts [128]).

Lipsyte continues: "I kind of liked that idea [about superpowers], and it evolved"—along with his emerging interests in the chemical poisoning of the environment, the cyberpunk science fiction novels of William Gibson, the Dungeons and Dragons games his son was playing, the visualization or imaging exercises that cancer patients employ to destroy cancerous cells, and his long-standing concern about athletes' casual drug abuse to expand their bodies and enhance their performance. All of these issues ultimately found their expression in *The Chemo Kid*, which Lipsyte, with some justification, calls his "most intricate book," adding that "it took a long time for everything to be digested." It took a long time and a great deal of rewriting, as well.

In fact in its multiplicity of themes, *The Chemo Kid* may remind some readers of Lipsyte's earlier novel, *Jock and Jill*, a similarity the author seems to wish to reinforce by setting both books in the same suburban community: Nearmont, New Jersey. The high school coach, the ham-fisted Coach Burg, is a character in both novels, and both also deal with the issue of drug abuse by high school athletes, though in *The Chemo Kid* the treatment of the issue will be invested with an intriguing comic-book sensibility commensurate with Fred's arguable status as a superhero.

Lipsyte concurs with this notion: despite its serious purpose of giving hope to real-life chemo kids, "I think it's pretty clear early on that you don't have to take this as a 'realistic' novel, by any means." Consider, for example, how the sensitive drug-abuse issue is introduced: After Mara discovers Fred's lump while they are dancing at the Junior Prom, Fred rushes to the bathroom to find a mirror. Instead he finds a surreal scene: the captain of the football team, Tank Ganz, and most of his players are lined up against the wall with their tuxedo pants down around their ankles. They are passing around a bottle and howling in pain while the high school drug dealer, Roger Sharkey, and his "twin goons" jab hypodermic needles into their "white and pink and brown backsides."

Even Fred cannot believe what he is seeing: "Not real life. A dream, a TV movie, the start of a new CyberPunk Rovers adventure?" (6). Any one of these alternative realities will serve as a paradigm for the kind of quirky distance that separates this novel from the grittily realistic fiction Lipsyte had written previously. In fact, the author suspects that some of the criticism that greeted the book's publication in 1992 was due to reviewers' belief, as he puts it, "that I'm supposed to write realistic street books, and I have no right to do other stuff."

By choosing to let Fred tell his own story as a first-person narrator, Lipsyte allows additional latitude for unreality or, at least, ambiguity in his treatment of Fred's superpowers, a fact he relishes. "Did he go nuts from the drug?" Lipsyte mused in an interview. "Maybe. Maybe it's a dream. Maybe he's dead already. Maybe it really did happen. There's some element of mystery to all of this."

The mystery and ambiguity enter the narrative with Fred's recovering consciousness after the surgical removal of his tumor. Though he intuitively knows that his prognosis is bad, he is oddly unafraid. "It all seemed unreal, a CyberPunk Rovers adventure" (28). This is a reference to a computer game that he and his friends had fervently played several years before. The game is Lipsyte's nod to William Gibson's post-apocalyptic Cyberpunk world: "The adventures took place in a high-tech future run by multinational corporations that killed for information."

The Rovers are hustlers "operating on the Edge, slipping in and out of dangerous deals with the corporations and the Stilyagi [an international crime organization]" (19). Each player creates an alter-ego Rover persona in the game. Significantly, Fred's is Ranger, "a white hat hero in a world of greys. Ranger never quit . . . But Ranger always died" (25). The world of the game assumes increasing importance in the book as an analogue to the "real" world; indeed, when it becomes obvious to Fred that all of the people he encounters have counterparts in the game, he thinks, "I was going crazy. Reality and fantasy had finally merged" (137).

The idea that Fred *might* be going crazy has already been planted in the reader's mind when Fred asks, "Can you go crazy from chemo?" and his doctor cautiously confirms that patients may have "hallucinations or delusions" (45). This invites the reader to speculate that Fred's reports of his superpowers (he throws a 300-pound barbell at a mirror, for example) are, in fact, hallucinations. This possibility is reinforced by the routine efforts of other characters, including his doctor, to rationalize these episodes as the work of his imagination.

As Fred's "powers" continue to develop and as the line between reality and fantasy continues to blur, Fred realizes that Ranger, at least, is no longer the hero he needs. "This is no job for Ranger. He was a fantasy character in a kid's game. This is for real. This is a job for The Chemo Kid" (138).

The job in question is to collect samples from a mysterious plant adjacent to the local reservoir to prove that the owners, Sinclair Ecosystems, are dumping toxic wastes into the community's water supply (there is a suggestion that this may be what has given Fred his cancer). The raid on the plant assumes the "real life" form of a CyberPunk Rovers game (Fred even thinks, at its outset, "The Game had begun") but it has, as its catalyst, Mara's realistically presented ecological activism. Earlier in the book she has announced to Fred, "This planet has cancer, and if people like you and I [*sic*] don't do something together, there's no hope" (75).

If the CyberPunk Rovers game offers a parallel universe, it is only one of many parallels that the reader encounters in Lipsyte's "most intricate" book. As previously noted, all of the characters have parallel personas in the Game. Additionally, Fred has cancer; the planet has cancer. Fred takes drugs; the football team takes drugs. And there are parallels, as well, to Lipsyte's earlier books, starting with the Nearmont setting and the issue of drug abuse that parallels *Jock and Jill*. As noted, the neanderthal Coach Burg is a character in both books (and is still discreetly looking the other way when his players take drugs). The name Sinclair Ecosystems is borrowed from Roger Sinclair, the villain of *The Summerboy*. A minor character is named Laura *Marino*, a surname borrowed from the "Summer" trilogy. Bobby's superpowers are described as "cold fire," a phrase borrowed from *The Contender*; his powers make his senses "super sharp" like those of a Running Brave from *The Brave* and *The Chief*. The strategy for the raid on Sinclair Ecosystems is borrowed from an old Cary Grant movie, a device that Bobby Marks would have relished; similarly Fred thinks, "I tried to remember how the hero did it in old movies . . . Bogart in *Casablanca*." Mara is doing a term paper on heroes in literature as Bobby did in *The Summerboy*. Fred thinks of his basement sanctuary as his "cave," à la Alfred and James in *The Contender*.

The most substantive parallel, however, is the principal theme, the transformation of self, which has informed virtually all of Lipsyte's earlier fiction. If there is a difference, it is that Fred is "assisted" in his transformation by the experimental drugs he is taking, unlike Alfred Brooks, Bobby Marks, and Sonny Bear, all of whom transform themselves through sheer hard work and the even more taxing exercise of their wills. On the other hand, there is evidence that Fred is himself instrumental in his transformation into his own hero when he chooses to defy the villains and put himself into jeopardy to help Mara in her righteous fight against environmental pollution. As Dr. Wallabini observes, "There are many cases of patients believing that the chemotherapy is doing more than destroying cells. It is part of the process by which patients gain control by reinventing themselves" (117).

The doctor, of course, is referring to more prosaic visualization exercises in which patients create mental images of their drugs seeking and destroying their cells. One of the other teenagers in Fred's support group, for example, visualizes his chemo as "a greaseball biker posse." "You've got to be your own hero," Wallabini has explained. "People need to find things inside themselves they never knew were there" (29).

Fred's particular triumph is not only to defeat cancer (there is no evidence of disease by the book's end) but in the process also to physically transform himself into a superhero with superpowers. And, what is more, to choose at the book's end to keep those powers, even though it means remaining bald and swollen and green. When Dr. Wallabini protests, "I can't leave you like this," Fred replies, "What about other kids with cancer?" (166). Lipsyte obviously intends his protagonist, radically empowered by his recovery, to serve as a symbol of hope for all young readers who have cancer. Fred's emergence as the Chemo Kid is, therefore, a powerful metaphor for the individual's heroic struggle against life-threatening disease. It can also be appreciated as the central conceit for Lipsyte's only experiment (to date) with speculative fiction, which, in style and tone, mixes elements of cyberpunk science fiction, melodrama, magical realism, and superhero comic book literature. In fact, Lipsyte himself describes *The Chemo Kid* as "a comic," that is, a comic book—a notion that is reinforced when one of Fred's friends says, "Isn't life a comic book?" (61) and when Lipsyte describes his melodramatic villains as being "just cartoony enough that we wouldn't have to deal with them as real people." The villains, like cancer itself, represent undiluted antagonism to the good, whether that is Fred, his health, or the health of the planet.

The infusion of this comic-book sensibility affords the reader and—one suspects—the author some necessary emotional distance from the intensity of the subject matter. Lipsyte was fighting his own second bout with cancer at the time he was writing this book, which explains why he describes it as being his most cathartic—more so, even, than *One Fat Summer*: "I cried while I was writing it . . . more than [with] any other book."

Despite this air of emotional intensity, *The Chemo Kid* is full of humor (Lipsyte wryly calls it "a cancer comedy"), but it is of an idiosyncratic type that the author dubs "tumor humor." Its most important attribute is the fighting attitude it epitomizes that is necessary to survive a trip to CancerWorld "because it keeps you loose. But it's tricky. Tumor humor is not warm and friendly; it does not necessarily release feel-good endorphins . . . Tumor humor is scrappy and sometimes nasty and tasteless, a sort of chemotherapy for the spirit—necessary but never nice."[2] An example of tumor humor is Fred's response when his friends ask him about his stay in the hospital: "It's just like high school only you vomit more" (37). The infusion of this brand of humor into the text is necessary not only to lighten its emotional intensity but also to lend verisimilitude, since "tumor humor" is a fixture of real-world cancer wards. Lipsyte recalls that "some of the funniest stuff I've ever heard was on the hospital's urology floor."

The problem with this type of humor is that, as both Lipsyte *and* Fred explain, "it's a location joke—you have to be there" (142). For those who are there, it is the glue that bonds them together into the kind of cohesive group which Fred encounters in his hospital therapy group, "Wallabini's Weenies," and which finds its analog in the CyberPunk Rovers' "Mutant Pack." "That's the Pack," Fred says. "They could save you, they could kill you. The rowdy mutants were always the wild cards in the deck. But they were the only cards I had" (140).

Like any newcomer, Fred has to prove himself to the therapy group/Pack. After a series of false starts, he finally does this by telling them about the emergence of his superpowers: "I told the whole story at shrink-rap, from the beginning, as if it were a CyberPunk Rovers adventure, no personal feelings, just action . . . I'd never had such an attentive audience before . . . I liked their silence, the way their eyes were locked on me" (115).

Once Fred wins the acceptance of the group, he also wins its staunch support when he and Mara take on Sinclair Ecosystems. The Pack's spirit of swashbuckling panache adds a welcome edge to Fred's adventures, but its friendship may be even more important to the book in terms of contributing to Fred's personal growth. Lipsyte notes that, as a cancer patient, he was never a member of a group as formally organized as Fred's but recalls that he and other patients "evolved our own group. It was kind of a travelling group—a bunch of us would walk around pushing our IV carts and talking and helping the younger guys through the next moment." The experience took Lipsyte into another world with its own unique sense of community and perspective of reality, and he philosophically credits cancer with being "yet another guide [like Dick Gregory and Oren Lyons] into this other world."

This "other world" of cancer, or any other potentially terminal disease, is suffused with unreality (beginning with the first stage of the patient's denial) and, yes, magic. Even the phrase "magic bullet" has passed into common usage to describe a drug or treatment that cures a disease. Fred's experimental hormone treatment can certainly be viewed as such a magic bullet: "It persuaded your natural defenses to exert superhuman effort," Dr. Wallabini crows (164). And in the process, of course, it also *magically* transformed the patient into a superhero—if we are to accept Fred as a reliable narrator—whose superpowers are finally as obvious to everybody as is his startling resemblance to "The Incredible Hulk" of television and comic book fame. It is equally obvious by the book's end that Fred's fully emergent superhero status signifies not only the defeat of cancer but its unconditional surrender. Sinclair Ecosystems and its allies in the corrupt local power structure—the Mayor and Chief of Police—are similarly routed and the high school villains are forced to reform. As for Fred? "It's a big world"; he thinks, "there's lots to do. And I don't even know yet what the Chemo Kid could become capable of doing" (167).

Knowing Lipsyte, one suspects we will find out in a sequel. Earlier we have read this exchange between Fred and his friend Vandal: Vandal says,

> Any time, Chemo Kid, any place, for any reason you need me, just call.
> "You're the leader of the pack," I said.
> "And the Pack will be back." (162)

As previously suggested, the reviews for *The Chemo Kid* were mixed. While generally praising the author's "rare blend of sensitivity, boisterous humor, and wry awareness of various political undercurrents,"[3] many reviewers had trouble with what they perceived as the "abrupt" shift from the realism of the first half of the novel to the fantasy and "wish-fulfillment" of its second half.[4]

The more compelling question of whether Fred's personal triumph over cancer would have been more emotionally satisfying in the context of a realistic novel was not addressed by the reviewers. Nor was the question of whether his emergence as a cartoonish superhero is ultimately more arresting than his almost incidental victory over his disease. This is a central issue in a book whose ostensible purpose is to celebrate the individual's realistic capacity to survive.

On the other hand the book's thought-provoking capacity even to raise such questions and invite such debate may be perceived as one of its great strengths. As a work of fiction, moreover, it is one of Lipsyte's most compulsively readable and exciting books. In its humor, its challenge to the imagination, and in its daring departure from his typical form it is, inarguably, as one reviewer concluded, "an attention-getter, and every reader will cheer Fred on."[5]

Superstar Lineup

In his next project, Lipsyte has returned not only to realism but to nonfiction. He has ambitiously set out to write "a history of the twentieth century through the lives of major sports figures" ("Listening," 295). Thus far, two books in this series, which his publisher, HarperCollins, is calling Superstar Lineup, have been published: *Jim Thorpe: 20th Century Jock* and *Arnold Schwarzenegger: Hercules in America* (both published in 1993).

Lipsyte's choice of subjects for his first two volumes is wonderfully consistent with the interests and thematic concerns evidenced in all of his previous work. In the book about Native American athlete Jim Thorpe, whose career was marred by prejudice and misunderstanding, Lipsyte has found a perfect forum for his social concerns and hatred of social inequity. And in Schwarzenegger he has found a real-life person whose character and career have been distinguished by a peerless capacity for self-invention and self-transformation.

Lipsyte's decision to undertake the writing of a series of sports biographies is a bold one, given his outspoken criticism of the failings of the form. He believes that it perpetuates the same kinds of meretricious myths that popular sports fiction does: "If you're willing to take orders, if you're determined to succeed, everything else will work itself out. Blacks and whites will get together, the coach will be understanding, poor kids will get rich, and the team will win the championship" (Miles, 45).

Such pleasant fantasies are notably absent from *Jim Thorpe*. First of all, the book is rooted in factual history. It begins with the first Native American athletes, the running braves. "They bound their world together with their savvy and their speed," Lipsyte claims, "as diplomats and messengers" (2). As for their descendent, Jim Thorpe: he "was a spirit of his time, a symbol of a country flexing its muscles in the world arena, a person who would not be beaten down; he was an athletic pioneer, but he also followed a path blazed by centuries of Runners for the Nation. The message he carried was his own story" (5).

Lipsyte makes it clear that Thorpe was born at a time (1887) when Native Americans were routinely demonized as "bloodthirsty Redskins" and dehumanized as "a form of wildlife in the way of growth and profit" (15). Like Sonny Bear, however, Jim Thorpe was half-white and his parents "apparently tried to give their children the best of both Indian and white cultures . . . In later years, Jim would be able to move easily in both worlds" (17–18). Or as easily as any Native American could, given Lipsyte's stated premise that "long after the battle for territory had ended, the battle for human rights and ethnic identity raged on. And still does" (55).

Despite these odds Thorpe became the first "global" sports star, thanks in part to his extraordinary abilities in every sport he tried and in part to the talents for public relations and publicity of "Pop" Warner, his coach at the Carlisle Indian School. Ultimately, however, his coach would betray him in the wake of the 1912 Olympic Games—which had been a triumph for Thorpe in the pentathlon and decathlon—when it was revealed that he had earlier played for money in semi-professional baseball. Warner drafted a letter for Jim to sign admitting his alleged guilt and implicitly accepting all responsibility. Warner, Carlisle, and the U.S. Olympic Committee were exonerated, but Thorpe was stripped of his medals and trophies and his name was expunged from the Olympic record books.

Chief Oren Lyons, Lipsyte's "guide" to the Native American world, believes this was a particularly egregious example of white injustice to Native Americans: "The white world had to beat him down because he was so strong," Lyons tells Lipsyte. "Jim Thorpe showed up the white world," he continues. "They were trying to prove we were savages; how else could they justify stealing our land and killing us? But here was Jim Thorpe and this raggedy group of savages from Carlisle, who just recently had their hair cut, just recently got shoes, and they're whipping West Point and Harvard. The white world took it as an insult. They had a respect for us in a way, but they had to beat us down" (90).

For Lipsyte, Thorpe's enduring legacy is the symbol he offers of the Native American's capacity to triumph in the face of such white injustice.

He tries to find similar symbolic value in the life and career of bodybuilder, actor, and superstar Arnold Schwarzenegger, but his claim that "he was a symbol for those who wanted authority and control over their bodies and their politics" seems strained.[6]

However, there is no question, based on what the author has shown us of Schwarzenegger's single-minded climb to the top, that he is a model of almost superhuman self-discipline, particularly in terms of training. Aside from hearsay and the popular perception of Schwarzenegger as "Conan the Republican," Lipsyte offers little hard evidence of "Arnold's" value as an authoritarian symbol in the political arena, however.

Indeed, if these relatively brief books have a failing as biographies, it is their overreliance on hypothesis. One of the most often used words in *Jim Thorpe* is "maybe" while in *Arnold Schwarzenegger* it is the phrase: "It is not hard to imagine." There is obviously much about any subject's life that a biographer cannot know for a fact, but the overreliance on the subjunctive ultimately tends to undermine the reader's confidence in the author's authority, particularly, as in the case of these two books, where there is no attribution, little citation of sources, and a strong authorial point of view. The reader comes away from these two books with the conviction that Lipsyte venerates Thorpe and dislikes and distrusts Schwarzenegger. And yet, at less than a hundred pages of text each, there is simply not enough material, enough reporting of illuminating incident to support this point of view. This lends these two volumes an almost perfunctory, going-through-the-paces air, as if the author has lost his interest in his subjects and his energy in telling the story of their lives.

On the other hand, Lipsyte clearly tries very hard—and successfully—to establish the context for these two lives in order to show how his subjects' early environments (both at home and in society) contributed to the formation of their adult characters, whether it is an evocation of the white majority's attitude toward "redskins" or Schwarzenegger's father's unforgiving attitude toward his younger, uncharismatic son, Arnold.

Despite these drawbacks, the two books have been well reviewed. *Publishers Weekly* called them "thoughtful works" that offer "balanced portraits of memorable individuals."[7] And Daniel Menaker, writing in the *New Yorker*, praised the Schwarzenegger biography for its "balanced view" and for introducing young readers to "psychological complexity."[8]

Two other biographies in this series—of basketball great Michael Jordan and boxer Joe Louis—have been published.

11. Still a Contender

"The most fun that I've had in my life is writing."

Reflecting on his career as a writer, Lipsyte recently said, half-jokingly and half-seriously, "You know, making a living has really interfered with my writing a lot." By this, of course, he meant that the daily requirements of writing newspaper and magazine columns, of being a broadcast journalist, of hosting a television program, of teaching, of traveling in search of stories to report, of writing magazine and newspaper articles—all the business of working as a "writer for hire" to support his family—have distracted him from his other career as a novelist. "I started out as a kid thinking of myself as a fiction writer, not as a journalist," he reflected. "The single happiest professional time I can remember was writing a book called *Liberty Two* when I had enough of an advance to do nothing for a year but work on the book every day."

On the other hand Lipsyte is quick to recognize the positive impact his life as a journalist has had on his fiction writing: "Journalism does not help in writing fiction," he flatly asserts, "but in terms of experience of life or learning, it has been invaluable. I've always seen journalism as a way for a basically shy person to get out and meet people and see what's going on. The fact that I get out more is probably the only difference between me and most other young adult writers." Indeed, one wonders how many other young adult authors could report, as Lipsyte did in a recent telephone conversation, that he had just returned from "driving around the South Bronx distributing sandwiches and condoms to prostitutes with AIDS."

Lipsyte values his "real life" experiences, which have obviously enriched such novels as *The Contender, Jock and Jill,* and the two Sonny Bear books, while providing the very substance of *Assignment Sports* and *Free to Be Muhammad Ali*. However, he also feels that the amount of time he must give them, time he cannot give to his fiction, has made him "a lesser writer." He explains: "I've got a lot of areas that I would like to improve—description, setting scenes—and that I'm trying to work on. If I were writing all the time, I probably would advance more quickly."

Aside from getting him out of the house, Lipsyte's experience as a journalist has influenced his work more than he may realize. It certainly has made him a trained observer and an accurate reporter of telling detail, which, as has been previously noted, makes his novels models of verisimilitude. Additionally his fondness for metaphor as a shorthand literary device that can save a writer paragraphs of description, his use of short, declarative sentences, his brief, often self-contained chapters all surely derive from his work as a journalist and especially as a columnist. Lipsyte's preferred method of writing fiction is to do a first draft in longhand using a pencil, a method, he says, that "allows you to slow down and get into your head." Before the advent of the computer, however, this was too time consuming and, accordingly, most of his books were written on the typewriter—another hallmark of the working journalist. "The problem with that," he asserts, "is that I was a very fast typist and the staccato rhythm affected the rhythm of my writing."

There was also the practical problem with the typewriter of what he calls "the fatigue factor"—that is, the labor-intensive necessity, when rewriting, of having to retype a whole page or chapter. "It was deadly," he groans. Now, however, he uses the computer for rewriting, a process he "loves." ("I love to rewrite. I love to rewrite," he enthuses.) The computer accelerates this process to the point where he now has enough time to permit "the luxury of doing the first draft in pencil."

With some exceptions. *The Chemo Kid,* for example, was written directly on the computer. If there is, indeed, to be a sequel to *The Chief,* Lipsyte is toying with the idea of dictating the text.

His reasoning: "Marty is now writing strictly for the screen, so *he's* just taping. And it might be kind of fun to see what comes of it."

Because "fun" for Lipsyte is equated with "keeping moving and doing different things," it is no surprise that the process of "becoming" (that is, changing and growing) has been an overarching theme of all of his young adult fiction. He expands on this: "What I don't think I understood until I was middle-aged was that if you're very lucky, you're an adolescent forever, at least in the sense that you're still in the process of becoming. I find that I'm surprised by myself: as much as I want to say, 'This is the way I am,' I find that I'm still changing and in the process of becoming something else. I haven't settled yet, which, in some ways, is kind of scary. But that's the route I've chosen."

His willingness to try new things brought him into the field of young adult literature in the first place, not only as a fresh, new voice but as an innovator, a genuinely seminal figure in the emergence of realistic young adult fiction that, in its honesty and integrity and willingness to deal with hard-edged, sociopolitical issues, made the literature relevant to the lives, interests, and concerns of adolescents everywhere.

Although he professes to have known virtually nothing about young adult literature when he entered the writer's ring with *The Contender*, Lipsyte has since formed strong opinions about the field. Some of these were expressed in a 1986 article in the *New York Times Book Review*. In it he voiced his concern that the economic imperatives of bottom-line-directed publishing were turning excellence to mediocrity: "The best of YA, the quality novel that is not immediately commercial, may be an endangered species."

To Lipsyte, "in the best of YA, fully-realized characters, who happen to be adolescents, struggle through the process of *becoming*—often having to deal realistically with various aspects of sexuality, chemical dependency, illness, family dynamics, discrimination. Pat, happy endings are scorned, although there is usually some hope for a brighter future."[1] In a recent interview he expanded on his ideas about young adult literature: "There are certain responsibilities for writers within that genre that I'm not sure writers for adults have, and they are not dissimilar to the responsibilities that teachers or clergy or anybody in positions of moral authority have. Most importantly you have a responsibility not to lie. After that you can take them [young readers] on any trip you can take them on."

This said, he does allow some personal ambiguity about the writer's "moral responsibility" regarding hope and the arguable necessity for a happy ending in a young adult book: "Does Robert Cormier have a 'right' to present a world with no hope? Maybe not. I mean, where I'm coming from I don't believe it's true. Of course there's hope. You're alive, there's hope. So I don't know that you have the right to give that kind of bleakness to a child."

Lipsyte's own version of hope is typically expressed in his characters' demonstrated capacity to change their circumstances—or themselves—for the better. This message has posed a problem only once, he allows, and that was in terms of the original ending of *The Chemo Kid*; in it Fred chose to continue his chemotherapy for the sake of keeping his superpowers. When it was pointed out to Lipsyte that this might be interpreted as a metaphor for promoting drug use, he changed the ending. In the final version, when Dr. Wallabini announces, "I will immediately begin a new course of drugs for you" (165), Fred "just says 'no'" even though that will mean remaining green, bald, and bloated.

By the same token, the various changes that have visited his own life and brought with them certain attendant uncertainties (including the problematic outcome of his bouts with cancer) may explain Lipsyte's fascination with the continuity offered by sequels and his reluctance to say "good-bye" to any of his characters, including his villains. "I even wonder about Stick, the drug dealer," he admits. "I wonder what happened to him in prison."

"There is no real relief at the end of a book," he continues. "It's like being forced to leave your neighborhood. I would feel very sad if I couldn't go back and visit my characters." There is no question that, for Lipsyte, these characters have a life independent of the page. Ask him, for example, what will happen to Bobby (now "Professor") Marks, and his detailed answer suggests that he has just finished a phone conversation with the character: "Well, my concern is that he's going to rip Marty off. You can't trust writers. And there's no reason to suspect that he doesn't write a novel about a black kid and a half-Indian fighter that not only does well but also wipes out any possibility of Martin's book getting published."

Having said this, Lipsyte launches a defense of Bob: "Bobby needs this novel. Marty's got a lifetime in my other books. But I think that Bobby is in a real tough spot, and he needs to get over it, and he needs to get over it right now, and if this does it for him, fine. Sure, Bobby is probably exploiting Marty but, then, Alfred probably exploited Sonny. I mean, if these are going to be real people, let them be real people!" Lipsyte's obvious passion for his characters and for sharing their reality with his readers is among the most memorable aspects of his fiction.

For Lipsyte the last three years have been turbulent with change. His PBS series was canceled on short notice; he returned to the *New York Times*, began writing a monthly column for *American Health* magazine; had a second bout with cancer (his quip about this—"At least I don't have to worry about a subject for my column"—is vintage tumor humor); remarried (his third wife, Katherine Sulkes is a television producer who, like Lipsyte, worked on *Sunday Morning*); and returned to young adult literature—at approximately the same time that his publisher, Harper and Row, was purchased by media baron Rupert Murdoch, an acquisition that is still changing the corporate image and mentality of the venerable house—*and* his longtime editor, the distinguished Charlotte Zolotow, retired.

For the time being Lipsyte may find his only continuity in his work. He feels himself "amazingly lucky" to be back at the *New York Times* at a period when "my generation of copy boys, these good, old friends are in charge" (particularly because he admits he has a problem dealing with authority figures). Most recently he has begun doing a second column for the *Times*: a "cityside" column called "Coping" that, in its freewheeling scope, recalls his 1977 column for the *New York Post*—an experience he calls his "favorite" to date in print journalism. He is talking about doing another book about Sonny Bear and Martin Witherspoon, and at least two more books in his new series of sports biographies will be published. There may be other young adult novels, as well, if, to paraphrase him, his publisher feels there is a market for them (he is particularly interested in writing about the issue of sexual identity and sexual orientation in sports).

One hopes, of course, for more fiction from Lipsyte, but even if it is not forthcoming, his place as a seminal figure in the evolution of modern young adult literature will remain unchallenged. That all of his novels for young adults are still in print is final evidence that his books are as fresh and as timelessly relevant as when they were written.

Move over Alfred Brooks, Bobby Marks, and Sonny Bear: Robert Lipsyte is still a contender.

Notes and References

1. Becoming a Contender

1. Robert Lipsyte, "Facets," *English Journal*, March 1987, 16; hereafter cited in text.
2. Robert Lipsyte, "Listening for the Footsteps: Books and Boys," *Horn Book Magazine*, May–June 1992, 292; hereafter cited in text as "Listening."
3. Robert Lipsyte, *The Contender* (New York: Harper Keypoint, 1993), 143; hereafter cited in text.
4. All otherwise uncredited quotations from Lipsyte are from an interview conducted by the author at Lipsyte's New York City home on 9 March 1993.
5. Robert Lipsyte, *The Chemo Kid* (New York: HarperCollins, 1992), 7; hereafter cited in text.
6. Nat Hentoff, Review of *The Contender*, *New York Times Book Review*, 5 November 1967, 64.
7. Sari Feldman, "Up the Stairs Alone: Robert Lipsyte on Writing for Young Adults," *Top of the News*, Winter 1983, 199.
8. Robert Lipsyte, *Assignment Sports* (New York: Harper & Row, 1970), 121; hereafter cited in text.

2. Becoming Robert Lipsyte

1. Robert Lipsyte, *SportsWorld: An American Dreamland* (New York, Quadrangle/New York Times Book Company, 1975), 3; hereafter cited in text.
2. Betty Miles, "Robert Lipsyte on Kids/Sports/Books," *Children's Literature in Education*, Spring 1980, 44; hereafter cited in text.
3. Sam Elkin, Review of *Assignment Sports*, *New York Times Book Review*, 31 May 1970, 14; hereafter cited in text.
4. Robert Lipsyte, *Assignment Sports*, Revised and expanded edition (New York: Harper/Trophy, 1984), 137; hereafter cited in text.

3. *Chasing the Dream*

1.   Pete Axthelm, Review of *Something Going*, *Newsweek*, 2 April 1973, 93B.

2.   Unsigned review of *Something Going*, *Booklist*, 1 April 1973, 741.

3.   Unsigned review of *Something Going, Kirkus Reviews*, 1 December 1972, 1376.

4.   Jon L. Breen, Review of *Something Going*, *Library Journal*, 1 March 1973, 764.

5.   John R. Coyne, Jr., Review of *Liberty Two*, *National Review*, 17 January 1975, 54.

6.   Unsigned review of *Liberty Two*, *Publishers Weekly*, 11 March 1974, 42.

7.   Jonathan Yardley, Review of *Liberty Two*, *New York Times Book Review*, 28 April 1974, 36; hereafter cited in text.

8.   R. Z. Sheppard, Review of *Liberty Two*, *Time*, 13 May 1974, E3.

9.   Garry Wills, Review of *SportsWorld*, *New York Review of Books*, 30 October 1975, 6.

10.   Zimmerman, Review of *SportsWorld*, *Newsweek*, 24 November 1975, 122; hereafter cited in text.

11.   Robert Lipsyte, *Free to Be Muhammad Ali* (New York: Harper & Row, 1978), 2; hereafter cited in text.

12.   Mel Watkins, Review of *Free to Be Muhammad Ali*, *New York Times Book Review*, 4 March 1979, 32.

13.   Leonard Maltin, *Leonard Maltin's Movie and Video Guide: 1992 Edition* (New York: Signet, 1991), 1094.

4. *The YA Writer Redux*

1.   Robert Lipsyte, *Jock and Jill* (New York: Harper & Row, 1982), 4; hereafter cited in text.

2.   George Plimpton, "Sports: How Dirty a Game?" *Harper's Magazine*, September 1985, 48.

3.   Kevin Kenny, "An Interview with Robert Lipsyte," *The VOYA Reader*, ed. Dorothy M. Broderick (Metuchen, N.J.: Scarecrow Press, 1990), 287; hereafter cited in text.

4.   John Leonard, Review of *Jock and Jill*, *New York Times Book Review*, 25 April 1982, 34.

5. One Fat Summer *At Last*

1.   Norma Klein, "Not for Teens Only," *The Nation*, 12 March 1983, 314.

2.   Robert Lipsyte, *One Fat Summer* (New York: Harper & Row, 1977), 1–2; hereafter cited in text.
3.   Robert Lipsyte, "Prisoner of Fat," *American Health*, July–August 1991, 32; hereafter cited in text as "Prisoner."

6. More Marks

1.   Stephen Krensky, Review of *One Fat Summer*, *New York Times Book Review*, 10 July 1977, 20.
2.   Jane Abramson, Review of *One Fat Summer*, *School Library Journal*, March 1977, 152.
3.   Robert Lipsyte, "Heartsounds,"*American Health*, December 1991, 31–32.

7. Of Rules and the Boy

1.   Robert Lipsyte, *Summer Rules* (New York: Harper & Row, 1981), 1–2; hereafter cited in text.
2.   *Fifth Book of Junior Authors & Illustrators*, ed. Sally Holmes Holtze (New York: H.W. Wilson Company, 1983), 197.
3.   Patty Campbell, "The Young Adult Perplex," *Wilson Library Bulletin*, March 1981, 530.
4.   Robert Lipsyte, *The Summerboy* (New York: Harper & Row, 1982), 4; hereafter cited in text.
5.   Robert Lipsyte, "Rancho Redux," *American Health*, September 1991, 26.
6.   Nilsen and Donelson in *Literature for Today's Young Adults* claim that the literary form of *One Fat Summer* is that of the classic romance.

8. TV Time

1.   John Leonard, "Southern Comfort," *New York*, 30 January 1989, 58.
2.   Mary K. Ruby, "Robert Lipsyte," *Authors & Artists for Young Adults*, ed. Laurie Collier (Detroit: Gale Research, 1991), 7:147.
3.   George Robinson, "The 24-Year Comeback," *Publishers Weekly*, 26 July 1991, 11.
4.   Robert Lipsyte, *The Brave* (New York: HarperCollins, 1991), 20; hereafter cited in text.
5.   Robert Lipsyte, "Lacrosse: All-American Game," *New York Times Magazine*, 15 June 1986, 29; hereafter cited in text as "Lacrosse."
6.   Robert Lipsyte, *Jim Thorpe: 20th Century Jock* (New York: HarperCollins, 1993), 78; hereafter cited in text.

9. Metafiction Man

1.   Robert Lipsyte, *The Chief* (New York: HarperCollins, 1993), 2; hereafter cited in text.
2.   Robert Lipsyte, "The Five-Mile Run," *American Health*, December 1992, 23.
3.   Tracy Kidder, "Facts and the Non-Fiction Writer," *Washington Post Book World*, 5 September 1993, 1.
4.   "Trump Sues Over Indian Casino Permits," *Los Angeles Times*, 4 May 1993, A16.
5.   "Once-Poor Tribe Awaits a Flood of Casino Profits," *New York Times*, 18 July 1993, Y15.

10. Battling the Beast

1.   Robert Lipsyte, "Rematch with the Dread," *American Health*, April 1991, 27.
2.   Robert Lipsyte, "Tumor Humor," *American Health*, March 1992, 28.
3.   Unsigned review, *Kirkus Reviews*, 1 April 1992, 467.
4.   Karen Hutt, Review of *The Chemo Kid*, *Booklist*, 1 March 1992, 1272.
5.   Ann A. Flowers, Review of *The Chemo Kid*, *Horn Book Magazine*, March–April 1992, 210.
6.   Robert Lipsyte, *Arnold Schwarzenegger: Hercules in America* (New York: HarperCollins, 1993), 61; hereafter cited in text.
7.   Unsigned review, *Publishers Weekly*, 27 September 1993, 65.
8.   Daniel Menaker, "Fuzzy," *The New Yorker*, 13 December 1993, 121.

11. Still a Contender

1.   Robert Lipsyte, "For Teen-Agers, Mediocrity?" *New York Times Book Review*, 18 May 1986, 30.

Selected Bibliography

Primary Sources

Novels

The Brave. New York: HarperCollins ("A Charlotte Zolotow Book"),
  1991; HarperKeypoint, 1993.
The Chemo Kid. New York: HarperCollins, 1992; HarperKeypoint, 1993.
The Chief. New York: HarperCollins, 1993.
The Contender. New York: Harper & Row, 1967; HarperKeypoint, 1987.
Jock and Jill. New York: Harper & Row ("A Charlotte Zolotow Book"),
  1982; Scholastic/Vagabond, 1983.
One Fat Summer. New York: Harper & Row ("An Ursula Nordstrom
  Book"), 1977; HarperKeypoint, 1991.
Summer Rules. New York: Harper & Row ("An Ursula Nordstrom
  Book"), 1981; HarperKeypoint, 1992.
The Summerboy. New York: Harper & Row ("A Charlotte Zolotow
  Book"), 1982; Bantam, 1984; HarperKeypoint, 1992.

Nonfiction

Arnold Schwarzenegger: Hercules in America. New York: HarperCollins,
  1993.
Assignment: Sports. New York: Harper & Row, 1970. Revised and
  Expanded Edition. New York: Harper/Trophy, 1984.
Free to Be Muhammad Ali. New York: Harper & Row ("An Ursula
  Nordstrom Book"), 1978.
Jim Thorpe: 20th Century Jock. New York: HarperCollins, 1993.

Short Story

"Future's File." In *Within Reach*, ed. Donald R. Gallo. New York:
  HarperCollins, 1993.

Books for Adult Readers

Liberty Two. New York: Simon & Schuster, 1974.
The Masculine Mystique. New York: New American Library, 1966.
Nigger (with Dick Gregory). New York: Dutton, 1964.
Something Going (with Steve Cady). New York: Dutton, 1973.
SportsWorld: An American Dreamland. New York: Quadrangle/New York Times Book Company, 1975; Quadrangle, 1978.

Screenplay

That's the Way of the World (also known as *Shining Star*). United Artists-Marvin, 1975.

Columns

New York Times, 1967–71, 1991–
New York Post, 1977
American Health, 1991–

Journalism

Articles/Reportage. *New York Times*, 1959–67. Additionally Lipsyte has been a regular contributor to the *New York Times Magazine* since 1961 and an occasional contributor to *The Atlantic, Coronet, English Journal, Esquire, Harper's, Horn Book, The Nation, New York Times Book Review, Newsweek, People Weekly, Reader's Digest, Sport, Sports Illustrated*, and *TV Guide*.

Articles and Essays

"Facets," *English Journal*, March 1987, 16.
"For Teen-Agers, Mediocrity?" *New York Times Book Review*, 18 May 1986, 30.
"Listening for the Footsteps," *Horn Book*, May–June 1992, 290.

Secondary Sources

Books and Parts of Books

Chevalier, Tracy, ed. *Twentieth-Century Children's Writers*. 3rd ed. Chicago: St. James Press, 1989, 597.
Collier, Laurie, ed. *Authors & Artists for Young Adults*. Detroit: Gale Research, 1991, 7:139.
Evory, Anne, and Linda Metzger, eds. *Contemporary Authors*, New Revision Series. Detroit: Gale Research, 1983, 8:329.

Gallo, Donald R., ed. *Speaking for Ourselves*. Urbana: National Council of Teachers of English, 1990, 122.

Gunton, Sharon R., ed. *Contemporary Literary Criticism*. Detroit: Gale Research, 1982, 21:207.

Holtze, Sally Holmes, ed. *Fifth Book of Junior Authors & Illustrators*. New York: H. W. Wilson Company, 1983, 196.

Nilsen, Alleen Pace and Kennth L. Donelson. *Literature for Today's Young Adults*. 2nd ed. Glenview: Scott, Foresman, 1985.

Olendorf, Donna, ed. *Something About the Author*. Detroit: Gale Research, 1992, 68:135.

Senick, Gerard J., ed. *Children's Literature Review*. Detroit: Gale Research, 1991, 23:199.

Articles

Feldman, Sari. "Up the Stairs Alone: Robert Lipsyte on Writing for Young Adults." *Top of the News*, Winter 1983, 198.

Plimpton, George. "Sports: How Dirty a Game?" *Harper's Magazine*, September 1985, 45.

Robinson, George. "The 24-Year Comeback." *Publishers Weekly*, 26 July 1991, 11.

Scales, Pat. "*The Contender* and *The Brave* by Robert Lipsyte." *Book Links*, November 1992, 38.

Simmons, John S. "Lipsyte's *Contender*: Another Look at the Junior Novel." *Elementary English*, January 1972, 116.

Spencer, Pam. "Winners in Their Own Right." *School Library Journal*, July 1990, 23.

Interviews

Kenny, Kevin. "An Interview with Robert Lipsyte." In *The VOYA Reader*, ed. by Dorothy M. Broderick. Metuchen: Scarecrow Press, 1990, 284.

Miles, Betty. "Robert Lipsyte on Kids/Sports/Books." *Children's Literature in Education*, Spring 1980, 43.

Selected Book Reviews

Arnold Schwarzenegger: Hercules in America
Menaker, Daniel. *The New Yorker*, 13 December 1993, 121.

Assignment: Sports
Booklist, 15 September 1970, 97.

Chaskel, Walter B. *School Library Journal*, May 1970, 97.

Elkin, Sam. *New York Times Book Review*, 31 May 1970, 14.

Kirkus Reviews, 1 May 1970, 520.

Sutherland, Zena. *Bulletin of the Center for Children's Books*, February 1971, 95.

Assignment: Sports. Revised and Expanded Edition
Booklist, July 1984, 1542.
VOYA, October 1984, 211.

The Brave
Kinsella, W. P. *New York Times Book Review*, 1 March 1992, 29.
Kirkus Reviews, 15 September 1991, 1225.
Morning, Todd. *School Library Journal*, October 1991, 146.
Ott, Bill. *Booklist*, 15 October 1991, 429.
Publishers Weekly, 30 August 1991, 84.
Schmidt, Gary D. *The Five Owls,* November–December 1991, 39.
VOYA, December 1991, 314.
Zeiger, Hanna B. *Horn Book*, March–April 1992, 209.

The Chemo Kid
Flowers, Ann A. *Horn Book*, March–April 1992, 210.
Hutt, Karen. *Booklist*, 1 March 1992, 1272.
Kirkus Reviews, 1 April 1992, 467.
Morning, Todd. *School Library Journal*, March 1992, 256.
Publishers Weekly, 6 January 1992, 66.
VOYA, April 1992, 32.

The Chief
DelNegro, Janice. *Booklist*, 1 & 15 June 1993, 1814.
Forman, Jack. *School Library Journal*, August 1993, 186.
Publishers Weekly, 24 May 1993, 89.

The Contender
Bulletin of the Center for Children's Books, May 1968, 145.
Cosgrave, Mary Silva. *Horn Book*, December 1967, 759.
Hentoff, Nat. *New York Times Book Review*, 5 November 1967, 64.
O'Neal, Susan. *School Library Journal*, November 1967, 78.
Sutherland, Zena. *Saturday Review*, 16 March 1968, 39.

Free to Be Muhammad Ali
Booklist, 1 October 1978, 303.
Kirkus Reviews, 15 November 1978, 1256.
School Library Journal, December 1978, 71.
Watkins, Mel. *New York Times Book Review*, 4 March 1979, 32.

Jim Thorpe: 20th Century Jock
Publishers Weekly, 27 September 1993, 65.

Jock and Jill
Booklist, 1 April 1982, 1014.
Bulletin of the Center for Children's Books, April 1982, 152.

Kirkus Reviews, 1 March 1982, 277.

Leonard, John. *New York Times Book Review*, 25 April 1982, 34.

Nevett, M. S. *VOYA*, August 1982, 34.

Publishers Weekly, 12 March 1982, 85.

School Library Journal, May 1982, 86.

One Fat Summer

Abramson, Jane. *School Library Journal*, March 1977, 152.

Booklist, 1 March 1977, 1015.

Bulletin of the Center for Children's Books, July 1977, 177.

Kirkus Reviews, 1 April 1977, 359.

Krensky, Stephen. *New York Times Book Review*, 10 July 1977, 20.

Newsweek, 18 July 1977, 92.

Publishers Weekly, 25 April 1977, 75.

Summer Rules

Booklist, 15 March 1981, 1023.

Bulletin of the Center for Children's Books, April 1981, 156.

Campbell, Patty. *Wilson Library Bulletin*, March 1981, 530.

Forman, Jack. *School Library Journal*, April 1981, 141.

Kirkus Reviews, 1 April 1981, 437.

McBride, W. G. *VOYA*, June 1981, 30.

Publishers Weekly, 15 May 1981, 63.

Smith, April. *New York Times Book Review*, 26 April 1981, 68.

The Summerboy

Booklist, 1 September 1982, 36.

Bulletin of the Center for Children's Books, September 1982, 15.

Dobbins, Timothy M. *VOYA*, February 1983, 38.

Flowers, Ann A. *Horn Book*, February 1983, 53.

Forman, Jack. *School Library Journal*, January 1983, 86.

Kirkus Reviews, 1 September 1982, 1001.

Klein, Norma. *The Nation*, 12 March 1983, 314.

McHargue, Georgess. *New York Times Book Review*, 14 November 1982, 48.

Publishers Weekly, 5 November 1982, 70.

Appendix: Awards and Honors

Books

The Contender: Wel-Met Children's Book Award, Child Study Association; ALA Notable Children's Book, 1940–1970; New Jersey Authors Award, 1978.

One Fat Summer: *New York Times* Best Book of the Year; ALA Best of the Best Books for Young Adults, 1966–1988; ALA Best Books for Young Adults.

The Summerboy: *Booklist* Editor's Choice.

The Brave: ALA Best Book for Young Adults; ALA Recommended Book for Reluctant Young Adult Readers.

Others

Dutton Best Sports Story Award: 1964, 1965, 1967, 1971, 1976.

Mike Berger Award from Columbia University for Distinguished Reporting, 1966.

Emmy Award for On-Camera Achievement, Academy of Television Arts and Sciences, 1990.

Index

Page numbers in italics refer to illustrations.

The Author

Formerly Director of Library and Community Services for the city of Beverly Hills, California, Michael Cart is a nationally known expert on books for young readers. From 1981 to 1991 he also coproduced and hosted the nationally syndicated cable television author-interview program *In Print*. Now a full-time writer and lecturer, Mr. Cart is a columnist for *Booklist* magazine and is the author of more than 250 articles and reviews, which have appeared in the *New York Times Book Review*, the *Los Angeles Times Book Review*, and numerous other literary magazines and professional journals. He is the author of *What's So Funny?*, a critical study of humor in American children's literature, and is currently writing a critical study of contemporary young adult literature. He has served as an adjunct professor at UCLA, and in 1992 he was the first Bradshaw Professor at Texas Woman's University. Mr. Cart lives in Los Angeles.

The Editor

Patricia J. Campbell is an author and critic specializing in books for young adults. She has taught adolescent literature at UCLA and is the former Assistant Coordinator of Young Adult Services for the Los Angeles Public Library. Her literary criticism has been published in the *New York Times Book Review* and many other journals. From 1978 to 1988 her column "The YA Perplex," a monthly review of young adult books, appeared in *Wilson Library Bulletin*. She now writes a review column on the independent press for that magazine, and a column on controversial issues in adolescent literature for *Horn Book* magazine. Campbell is the author of five books, among them *Presenting Robert Cormier*, the first volume in the Twayne Young Adult Author Series. In 1989 she was the recipient of the American Library Association Grolier Award for distinguished achievement with young people and books. A native of Los Angeles, Campbell now lives on an avocado ranch near San Diego, where she and her husband, David Shore, write and publish books on overseas motor-home travel.

6/27/95
5.0.